I first met Zach one Sunday when and I was getting ready to teach. He and offered me a program. On the gentle-spirited, smiling, proud dad. Empowering these two was Linda, a loving, joy-filled, prayerful mom and wife. Her joy and journey is revealed in this book as she points us to the image of God in her son.

James Liske
CEO, Prison Fellowship Ministries

Life is about story and this book is filled with stories that highlight the joys and heartaches of parenting. Each chapter opened our hearts to the "Larger-Story" God is telling through Zach's life. We were reminded that life involves choices; and we celebrated how Zach's family repeatedly chose hope and a positive attitude in the face of disappointment and discouragement. This book reminds readers how sacrificial love and living in community can become the pathway to the sacred things in life.

Tim + Anne Evans
REAL LIFE ministries, Colorado Springs, Colorado

I have had the pleasure of watching the life of this incredible family as Zach has grown up in our community. *Incredible* is the word I use, not because they have a child with Down syndrome, but because of the way their family has affected an entire community. Zach's involvement with his school system and Hope College has had an enormous impact on everyone around him. And Linda has influenced our students as an annual guest lecturer in my courses at Hope College by articulating the life of a parent with Down syndrome in a compelling way from a parent's perspective.

Now, in the context of this wonderful story, we can all peek into the life of a faithful family learning to grow together while raising a young man who matters, first because of who he is as a person, and second in the context of having a disability. You will love this story!

Steven Smith, Ph.D.
Professor of Kinesiology, Hope College

Linda Aalderink tells a real story, an honest story as a parent of Zach—who just happens to have Down syndrome. It is also a story of faith, hope and love. Zach's story is about faith that clings to God's promises that each of us, as parents, hold dear for our children. It is a powerful story of hope for parents in a future that holds so many question marks. And it is a love story because love transforms relationships. It allows Chef Zach's feast, cooked and eaten every Friday evening at 7:00 p.m. with seminary roommates, to poignantly remind them and us of another feast of love that binds us together.

Rev. Matthew Floding, D.Min.
Director of Field Education, Duke Divinity School

In our culture today, we look to professional athletes for inspiration. We want to see signs of God's activity and power in their achievements and testimonies. Instead, we should be looking at Zach and the Aalderink family! Zach's story shows that despite the challenges, God's plans are not hindered by Down syndrome, and that His goodness and faithfulness are not changed by an extra chromosome. I was moved by this book.

Jason Hanson
Kicker, Detroit Lions

Immeasurably
MORE

To Meghan,
You have a story to write, and I know God will lead you though. He shows us the way to live our lives... one step at a time. Abundant blessings over you & your family.

♡ Linda Auldanik
Eph 3:20-21

zach

Immeasurably
MORE

More Hope, More Joy

EMBRACING LIFE WITH DOWN SYNDROME

LINDA AALDERINK

(with contributions from many of the wonderful
people who have enriched Zach's life)

credo
house publishers

Published by Credo House Publishers,
a division of Credo Communications, LLC, Grand Rapids, Michigan.
www.credohousepublishers.com

ISBN: 978-1-935391-88-3

Cover and interior design by Sharon VanLoozenoord

Printed in the United States of America

To my husband, Rick:
So glad we could take this journey together.

To Zach, Ben, and Kassi:
Truly an honor and privilege to be your mom.

To Dad and Mom, aka Norm and Norma:
Thanks for the unconditional love and support
you have always given.

To the memory of two of our town's finest:

Judy Kempkers
A wonderful and kind neighbor who encouraged
and guided us through a difficult chapter in our story.

Corla Kraker
Third grade teacher to all three of our kids
and one of our school district's very best.

CONTENTS

INTRODUCTION

"Heartache forces us to embrace God
out of desperate, urgent need.
God is never closer than when
your heart is aching."

JONI EARECKSON TADA

This is a story that needs to be told. It's about a journey—a journey of prayer, of hope, of laughter, and of God's amazing faithfulness. It shares stories and anecdotes from family, friends, teachers, and coaches.

It's a true story about the life of a young man whom God created in an "amazing and wonderful way" (see Psalm 139:14). If you're a parent, I'm confident you would say this about each of your children. They're all unique individuals, from their outward appearance right down to their inside "wiring." Yet as the years have gone by, I've observed with sadness that our culture and world don't see much, if any, value in a person who isn't "normal" or who was born with a disability—like perhaps an extra chromosome. But who gets to decide what "normal" is, anyway? The word can have an amazingly different connotation depending on who you ask.

Sadly, even in our "enlightened" day a woman who receives the news that the baby she is carrying has some anomaly, some "defect," may feel pressure, either from society in general or from particular individuals, to question whether her unborn baby's life has any value. The abortion rate for women who believe themselves to be carrying a child with Down syndrome is extremely high, between 50 and 90 percent. This is tragic. These women are either told or believe on the basis of a preconceived stereotype that there's nothing ahead but struggle and sorrow. My heart aches when I learn of women seeking abortions just because they're carrying a child with Down syndrome. Yes, there will be struggles, disappointments, and many new learning experiences, but isn't that the case for every baby who is born? If a baby is deemed "normal," do we really believe there will be no struggles ahead? I can personally attest that beyond the inevitable difficulties there is great joy—in fact, there's a very real potential for "over the top" joy, above anything they've experienced before, a joy that's pure and real.

As I write, I'm overwhelmed with joy at the goodness of God in giving our family Zach. His entry into our lives redefined us as a couple, as individuals, and as a family. In fact, I believe his life has helped to shape the hallways of our school, the sidelines of a local high school football game, and the community in which we live. As his mom, I can say with complete honesty that I'm truly thankful God picked me to be his mom.

As a 25-year-old woman expecting her first baby, was I hoping for this? Of course not! I didn't sign up for this seemingly huge speed bump. Women don't dream of having a baby with

Down syndrome. The fact is, though, that it's been a journey of blessing for which I'm incredibly thankful—a journey I wouldn't have missed for anything. I'll never forget the day my young teenage daughter made this profound observation: "Everybody needs a Zach in their life." I couldn't agree more. Our family has received much more from this special young man than we would ever be able to give back.

This book is written to encourage a primary audience of women who've been told they are or may be carrying a child with Down syndrome. If this is you, please hold on to the reality that you're posed to give life to a precious and beautiful creation. God has amazing plans ahead for both you and your baby. This baby isn't a mistake. God designed him or her for a grand purpose, a purpose yet to be revealed: "All the days ordained for me were written in your book before one of them came to be" (Psalm 139:16). My prayer is that you will read these stories and snippets from Zach's life and look forward to rearing your little one. You have ahead of you a rare and grand adventure, one you won't want to miss.

If you're already parenting a child with Down syndrome, I pray that these stories will enable you to see the potential in your little one. I pray that you'll see that it's okay to dream, to hope, and to ask. We serve a big God, One who can do infinitely more than we can even begin to imagine (Ephesians 3:20-21). These verses are the premise for the title *Immeasurably More*. God went inestimably beyond my own meager expectations. My encouragement to you: take one day at a time. Live in the moment, relishing every second. Days and years pass far too quickly. God will light your path . . . one step at a time.

For grandparents, families, and friends. I hope you enjoy the stories written by Zach's own siblings and friends. I pray these words will encourage you to stay involved or become more involved in the life of your family member or friend who has special needs. As I've looked at these relationships in our lives, I've learned that when people take the time to get to know Zach, when they go beyond what may be initially uncomfortable for them, they gain benefits. It is a win for both.

If you are a teacher, physician, or other professional, we parents simply ask that you see the value in our child. I pray that you can look beyond an educational label and a diagnosis and see the potential. All children with Down syndrome are not the same, each one is unique cognitively, physically, and emotionally. I appreciate professionals who show respect and treat Zach like the young adult that he is.

Pause to ponder, praise, and pray

"Now to him who is able to do immeasurably more
than all we ask or imagine, according to his power
that is at work within us, to him be glory in the church
and in Christ Jesus throughout all generations,
for ever and ever! Amen"
(Ephesians 3:20–21).

Now take a moment and pray this verse for—or even over—your precious child(ren).

"Do immeasurably more in _____'s life
than all we could ask or imagine, according to your
power that is at work within him/her. Glorify yourself
through his/her life, and for generations to come
(Ephesians 3:20–21)."

—from *Praying the Scriptures for your Children* by Jodie Berndt

CHAPTER 1

WHERE IT
ALL BEGAN

*"Faith goes up the stairs that love
has built and looks out the window
which hope has opened."*

CHARLES H. SPURGEON

This story begins in September of 1986. Ronald Reagan was president, IBM had introduced the first PC laptop, and America was spending its free time watching movies like *Top Gun* and TV shows like *Magnum PI* and *Dynasty*. My husband and I were eagerly anticipating the arrival of our firstborn. We had been married for four years and had recently moved into our brand new home. We're do-it-yourselfers, and the house was a project we had spent a busy year constructing. We now welcomed the new challenge of a baby and felt ourselves to be more than ready for this bundle of joy to arrive. The pregnancy had progressed in textbook fashion. Through all nine months, in fact, I considered myself the poster child for a "normal" pregnancy.

So as events unfolded on that September day, not one thing seemed unusual. I had no need to worry and was in fact prepared to savor the whole experience. After several hours of walking around the hospital floor, trying to rest between contractions while watching my husband eat the meals that were delivered for me, my labor was average, unspectacular.

In conjunction with the first signs of dawn, our baby boy put in his appearance. The anticipation over, we held him in our arms, gazing at him with awe and admiration. In the moments following Zach's birth we welcomed him with all the pent-up love and happiness we held within us. All was just as we had planned. We cuddled and kissed him and after a short while reluctantly handed over our precious bundle to the nurse for a bath and a checkup.

Energized by surging adrenaline, we began eagerly calling, spreading the exciting news to waiting family members in those early morning hours. First to hear were our parents; they wouldn't mind getting a call this early with such wonderful news, right? We gave them the details: weight, height, Apgar score, . . . all the important stuff. A bit later Rick drove home to get some rest and I settled in for a short nap. I was tired now, but I dreamed of what life would be like with a new baby in the family. Within an hour I realized that all of *my* planned scenarios were about to come crashing down.

Still in the early daybreak hours, the doctor on call for our pediatrician returned to my room and proceeded to inform me, seemingly without alarm, that Zach had a medical issue. The nurse who had attempted to take his rectal temperature had discovered that there was no opening for the thermometer. Our baby didn't have an anus opening, and the needed surgery wasn't something the doctors at our local hospital could do. There was no discussion— just the "matter-of-fact(s)."

I took everything in stride as best I could. I'd been up all night, of course, and by now was truly exhausted. Somehow I had to absorb the news that my sweet newborn had an urgent health problem. The doctors offered to discharge me for home. *Home? Are you serious? I just gave birth an hour ago! I can't go home while my baby goes to another hospital.* I asked whether I could also be transferred. Thankfully, the answer was yes. Within an hour or two my son and I were together discharged to a larger hospital in nearby Grand Rapids, Michigan. In my naivety, I felt as though I could handle the situation at hand. The medical issue could be corrected, and things still seemed simple enough.

It was only then that I called Rick, who already was home and drifting into the beginning of sleep, to inform him of the change in plans. We then had to call back our family members to advise them what was going on. Within an incredibly short time span Rick and I had been plunged from extreme happiness into the fear and uncertainty of the unknown. After a fairly straightforward childhood and young adulthood, I was getting my first dose of the reality that I wasn't in control of my life. God was, and His plan was beginning to play out differently from mine.

With all the paperwork for the transfer completed, Zach and I went for an ambulance ride—our first, thankfully, and hopefully our last. Strapped flat on my back to a gurney and wrapped in blankets, I felt like a mummy. Sweet baby Zach was in an incubator, and a nurse rode with us. I could see Zach lying in his little bed for the short 30 minute trip to Grand Rapids. Seemingly content, he didn't cry or fuss. Although I too lay quietly, thoughts raced through my head: *I hope this is a quick fix, so we can all go home soon. I wish they would unstrap me so I could lie on my side; my backside is killing me! This ambulance is really moving!* I could see out a small window at the bottom of the door and noticed that the yellow dashes on the pavement were flying along in the opposite direction at an alarming rate. There were no sirens, though, so how bad could this be? It didn't occur to me that this was going to be a big deal.

As I've pondered my initial, understated reaction, which I've had plenty of opportunity to do in hindsight, I'm astonished at my own naïveté. The transfer to a larger hospital via ambulance should have been a clue, but I wasn't getting it. Looking back, I believe this slow recognition was God's way of protecting me from the overload of TMI (too much information). The God of the universe always knows exactly what we need—and how much we can assimilate—on a moment-by-moment basis.

Upon our arrival in Grand Rapids, Zach and I went in opposite directions. My son was whisked away for tests, and at that point I had no idea what the doctors were checking for. I was admitted and brought to my room. It was on a floor for new moms, but all of our babies were in the Neonatal Intensive Care Unit (NICU). I saw Zach there about two hours later. It was at this point that reality began to flood in. In order to enter the NICU, both Rick and I had to wash our hands and arms thoroughly and wear those hospital gowns that don't close in the back, along with masks.

There was Zach in his incubator, with a tube down his nose, still seemingly contented. We could touch his body through little holes on the side of the incubator. His skin was petal soft, and he looked sweet and perfect in our eyes. Looked around the room we took in several other incubators, all holding babies— tiny, tiny babies, each weighing only a couple of pounds. Zach seemed in comparison like a Goliath, weighing in at a healthy seven pounds two ounces. Comparatively, he was huge! Unaccountably, that made me feel better.

By now it was mid afternoon. Zach's grandparents had arrived, and we were all awaiting news on his physical condition. I was in my hospital room, a floor or two away from the NICU, when Rick and I received a visit from a neonatologist. He explained that Zach had been born with an imperforate anus and that he would require surgery later on that same day. He went on to inform us that our beautiful son had two holes in his heart that would require medication and very likely open-heart surgery. He would need to be closely monitored during the months ahead. The third piece of information was that the doctors were quite sure Zach had Down syndrome. It was at this point that my mind was pleading *Please, just stop. The medical issues are enough. I have no idea what all of this really means. I can't deal with a disability too.*

We really didn't have much knowledge about Down syndrome, but as the neonatologist was talking images were popping, unbidden, into my mind, and I must admit they were less than positive or encouraging. The neonatologist told us that a blood test—a karyotype—would be done on Zach to determine what type of Down syndrome he had, if indeed he had the condition. The neonatologist asked whether we had any questions, to which we numbly shook our heads. There were questions, of course, a whole barrage of them, but we lacked the words to formulate or express them. What do you say to this kind of bombardment?

Our parents were in the hallway, anxiously waiting for answers, but our heads were spinning with the impact of the news itself, along with the overload of information we were attempting to absorb into our overstressed and tired brains. It felt as though I had just stepped off one of those dizzying rides at the fair. The doctor compassionately offered to share with our parents what he had just shared with us; we agreed and thanked him for the offer.

The two of us sat, numb. *This isn't at all what we had in mind! Serious health issues? Surgery today? A colostomy? What's a colostomy, and how's that going to work? A hole in his heart? Down syndrome? We definitely hadn't signed up for this—any of it! But he doesn't look like he has Down syndrome . . . .* Although we allowed ourselves to shift into a temporary denial mode, trying to convince ourselves that we couldn't see the "signs," our primary concern for that moment and that first overwhelming day was our little one's physical health and impending surgery. The Down syndrome could wait. We didn't want to think about it. Besides, they could be wrong. Doctors are only human, after all. This, at least, was our thought process.

All this news was difficult for the grandparents as well. In fact, I believe it was even harder for them to accept. It hit like a double whammy of hurt and disappointment; they weren't hurting just for us but for Zach as well. Coming from a generation where people with Down syndrome were called Mongoloids and were often sent away to institutions and kept out of schools, out of the public eye, their lack of familiarity with disabilities was even greater than our own.

We met others that day, doctors who would follow Zach for years to come. We remain heartily grateful for the skilled, knowledgeable, professional doctors and nurses God sent, already so early on, to care for Zach. Many have become friends and follow with interest Zach's progress in all areas of his life. God had prepared the way long before Zach had been born.

Zach was approximately 15 hours old that evening when he endured his first surgery. Rick and I gratefully received the news late in the evening that the operation had been successful. A colostomy had been put in place and seemed to be working. For that night, this was enough. We didn't lie awake, wondering what the future might hold. We rested. It felt as though we had been riding a rollercoaster all day long, and it was time to get off. I ordinarily relish a great rollercoaster ride, but it was time to stop. It was time for a break, and God graciously granted it to us in the form of a night's restorative sleep. Both Rick and I truly experienced the peace of God that transcends all understanding, guarding our hearts and minds in Christ Jesus (see Philippians 4:7).

On day two we began to see what a trooper our little Zach really was. He recovered from the surgery quickly and completely. He nursed, and he gained weight. This was all normal stuff. We received a visit from a kind woman from the Down Syndrome Association of West Michigan, an organization designed to support parents of children with Down syndrome. She showed us pictures of other kids and talked with us about the association and all it had to offer new parents. We listened and looked, but in my heart I was denying that this related to me. Sure, their kids were cute, and the families appeared happy and well adjusted. Still, I hoped that maybe, just maybe, the doctors were wrong. I wasn't going to deal with the diagnosis of Down syndrome until I knew for sure. I was going to wait until the official results were in.

Meanwhile, I spent my days visiting Zach in the NICU. Often we would just rub his arm or tummy through the incubator openings. It was a treat to occasionally be able to hold him, but also a little nerve-racking with all those attached tubes. The nurses encouraged me to try to nurse him, although they weren't sure whether he would have the sucking reflex or the strength to take his nourishment this way. At a few days old, though, he was already beating the odds and nursing just fine. To see how much milk he had actually taken in, Zach was weighed each time before he nursed and then again immediately afterward. Every detail was documented, and overall the doctors were pleased with his progress. He was healing and eating like a "normal" baby.

One day of our hospital stay was particularly memorable for me. We had received visits from friends, family members, and our pastor. I remember joining hands together and praying in my hospital room. It was in that moment that I realized I wasn't going to be able to do this alone. Rick and I, as a couple, couldn't do this alone. This was bigger than we could ever have imagined. Simply becoming a parent for the first time is an overwhelming and daunting proposition. Adding to the equation a child with extra needs and an uncertain future, we needed to give this situation, and more especially this child, to the Lord and seek His guidance on how to raise him. This was going to be a journey on many levels—spiritual, physical, emotional, and even intellectual. I wondered whether this outcome was the result of something I had done, or had failed to do, during the course of my pregnancy. This was my first taste of upheaval in my entire life, which had been comfortable and good for 25 years. Now it was time to really begin to trust God for our future. This was where the rubber met the road.

One day, while visiting Zach in the NICU, my eye was caught by the poem on a large poster on the wall:

Heaven's Very Special Child
by Edna Massionilla

A meeting was held quite far from Earth.
"It's time again for another birth,"
Said the angels to the Lord above.
This special child will need much love.
His progress may seem very slow
Accomplishments he may not show.
And he'll require extra care
From the folks he meets way down there.
He may not run or laugh or play;
His thoughts may seem quite far away.
In many ways he won't adapt,
And he'll be known as handicapped.
So let's be careful where he's sent,
We want his life to be content.
Please, Lord, find parents who
Will do a special job for you.
They will not realize right away
The leading role they're asked to play
But with this child sent from above

Comes stronger faith and richer love.
And soon they'll know the privilege given
In caring for this gift from Heaven.
Their precious charge, so meek and mild,
Is Heaven's very special child.

At the time two things struck me about this poem. First was the word "handicapped." It struck me as cold, harsh, complicated, overwhelming, and negative. Second was the thought that God picked parents who *could do* this special job. I wasn't entirely sure He'd made the right choice with me. There was so much unknown about Zach's, and our, future. How much of a future would he have? What would it be like? Where would he go to school? Would he have friends? Yet through this mad tumble of questions I knew that first and foremost Zach was a baby who needed love and care. That, I knew, we could provide.

The week at the hospital quickly passed. I was able to stay admitted for almost the entire time Zach was there, and I appreciated the close proximity to my son. I was discharged on a Wednesday, and the following day we returned to the hospital to bring our little Zach home. Grandpa and Grandma had gotten him an especially cute, soft blue sweater with a matching hat. Zach was simply adorable as we dressed him for the first time in "real" clothes. Now this was fun!

Zach began to thrive, and we knew that our hearts and lives would be changed in amazing ways from that day on. The biggest challenge during the first week at home was getting the colostomy bags to fit properly and learning how to care for our son's skin under the bag adhesive. This seemed overwhelming, and I remember the first full day home when visitors stopped by and I was in the bathroom crying.

Thankfully, the learning curve wasn't too long or steep; we adjusted and quickly became expert at caring for him and his colostomy. Our evenings were often spent watching our favorite television show while cutting out the colostomy bags to give a custom fit for Zach. Exciting! After a short time the fitting and cutting of these bags became no big deal. It was simply something we had to do. Zach was a sweet baby and a good sleeper, which helped tremendously. It can at times be astonishing to realize our real capabilities. How often we sell ourselves short, thinking "we can't" when in actuality we can.

Rick returned to work, and I enjoyed lots of visitors, all bearing gifts for the new little bundle. This was fun, and we quickly settled into a routine. While we waited for the "official" results of the chromosome test for Down syndrome, though, I remember feeling that the weather outside reflected my inner feelings. It was raining—a lot. The skies were gray, and the sun didn't shine. I remember my heart being heavy. There was much uncertainty about our future, how much we couldn't have begun to know. Honestly, I wasn't sure I wanted the whole truth, though I've learned since that anticipating the unknown is often more stressful than actually knowing and doing.

When Zach was around three weeks of age I received a call from the hospital. The results of his blood tests were in. The caller advised me, "He has Trisomy 21. It's the most common type of Down syndrome." The caller asked whether the hospital could do anything for me. My "No, thanks" was simple and controlled, and I quietly hung up the phone, thinking, *There, it's final.* The doctors had been right. In our hearts we had already known, so the diagnosis didn't throw us for a loop. Yet once the answer came it was as though we now had our "marching orders." We were already so in love with this absolutely precious baby God had given us that an extra chromosome would simply give us more to love. That may sound trite, but it was true. That extra chromosome that came with Zach was all part of the package, a package enfolding a gift that would keep on giving.

Gradually we learned more about this baby, and although ours wouldn't be the journey *we'd* had in mind, we trusted with all our hearts in the plan God had for this one-of-a-kind infant He had fashioned. The sun came out again too, heralding a breathtakingly brilliant autumn display. The sunshine lifted my spirits, and Zach and I were able to get outside to enjoy the color and warmth.

We had dear friends who had a baby girl just a month older than Zach. So we—the moms and babies—began taking walks together. This was therapeutic, both physically and emotionally. I must admit that negative thoughts would at times enter my mind—reawakened doubts about my ability to raise my own "special" child, envy over the perceived "ease" of raising a child without all of Zach's issues and the resultant uncertainty about his future. I'm thankful that these thoughts didn't linger . . . partly because I didn't permit myself to dwell on them. I believe that kind of thinking could have had an extremely negative impact on both Zach and me. My heart tells me in retrospect that even this too was evidence God's protective care: helping me dismiss those thoughts that were not from Him. I had much for which to be thankful, and I directed my thoughts toward those aspects of this new passage in my life.

From the very beginning, Rick and I always looked at Zach and saw . . . Zach! We never saw "handicapped." We didn't see Down syndrome. We treated him as we would have any other baby. He was our first; we were rookies who didn't know what to expect anyway. We allowed ourselves to expect that he could accomplish certain goals: sitting up, feeding himself, communicating, walking, and eventually talking. We knew it might take him a while longer, but we always believed he would do these things. Obviously he had some medical issues; he needed two meds each day for his heart, and he had a colostomy bag. These issues eased themselves into our routine. There were a few doctors we visited on a regular basis, but for the most part Zach was a sweet baby, and I was a blessed mom.

As I've looked back on how God took care of us through those early days, I've realized that His hand was also evident in the people He put in my path. Early on there was the babysitter. Prior to Zach's birth I had planned to return to my job on a part-time basis. We had recently built our home in Hamilton and had found a new church home in that community. Sally was someone I'd met at church. As my pregnancy progressed and I got to know her, I had asked her whether she would consider caring for our soon-to-be-born baby. She agreed, and arrangements were made for Sally to care for Zach on a part-time basis. After Zach was born, Sally never once expressed doubt about caring for this "special" little guy. She didn't waver in her commitment to care for him or verbalize misgivings about her ability to handle the situation. She took him in—heart medications, colostomy bags, extra chromosome and all; she just did it—and did it wonderfully!

I've been profoundly thankful for her unconditional acceptance of Zach, as though he weren't anything "special" but simply a little baby. Her acceptance affirmed for me that Zach was in so many ways "normal," and her response to him spoke volumes to me. At that time I don't believe I realized the impact her actions and attitude were having on me. But reflecting back on those early days, I acknowledge that knowing Sally made a significant difference in my outlook and attitude in caring for this "special" little guy. Sally's whole family grew to love Zach. Our families are still connected today, and a simple word of thanks seems unspeakably small for the huge impact Sally has had on our family.

At approximately six weeks of age Zach entered the Infant Program through the Ottawa Area Center. The idea of "early intervention" was relatively new at this time. The theory is to begin working with the special-needs babies as soon as possible so their development will be quicker and better. I remember my first appointment at the Center, the school for our area that is specifically designed for special-needs children, located 45 minutes from our home. While I waited in the lobby I looked at the trophy cases and pictures. Thinking about my little boy going to school, I knew in that moment that when Zach was old enough to attend school, I wanted Zach to attend the school in our home neighborhood, with his future siblings and the kids from our neighborhood, a school close to our home, not an hour (or more) bus ride away.

Through the Infant Program at the Center I met two women, the school nurse and the home trainer. Like Sally, both are examples of God providing just the right people to help get me started in the right direction and with the right outlook. They, like Sally, didn't make a big deal over Zach or his health issues. They simply taught me ways to care for him. The home trainer began coming to our home every week to work with Zach. As he gained strength and skills, I learned a lot from our weekly conversations. I looked forward to her visits and her encouragement on how well Zach was progressing. She was simply doing her job, but her impact went well beyond the benefits for Zach.

Our little boy remained healthy and continued to blossom. We had been seeing the cardiologist regularly since Zach's birth; he was monitoring the holes in Zach's heart, one of the more common health issues in kids with Down syndrome. At one year of age, exactly a week after Zach's birthday celebration, we were back at Spectrum Health Butterworth Hospital in Grand Rapids for Zach's open heart surgery. The feeling I had when I handed over this precious boy to the anesthesiologist was gut-wrenching, yet I somehow remained calm and peaceful. I watched him walk down the hallway holding Zach, and once again I placed my son securely in God's hands. We asked God to guide the surgeon's hands, and He did. Every hour throughout the surgery a nurse came out of the operating room and reported on Zach. He came through beautifully, healed quickly, and returned home only a week later.

Two months later we were back in the hospital, this time for reconstruction of Zach's imperforate anus. This was a longer visit, involving getting our son to drink castor oil in his bottle. I felt like the meanest mom in the world putting that stuff in his bottle. It was doctor's orders, though, and his colon needed to be cleaned. Once again the surgery was successful, thanks to the prayers of many people and the surgeon's skill. Zach again recovered quickly and was a model patient.

Only six weeks later Zach entered Butterworth yet again to reverse his colostomy, hook back up the internal plumbing, and wait for the poopy diaper. After the surgery we gave him bottle after bottle of apple juice to drink. Late one evening the big event occurred—the first ever dirty diaper! This was momentous and exciting—so much so that we called Grandpa and Grandma to share the good news. It's incredible how your perspective on "exciting" can change. This dream of a "perfect" baby was really beginning to take shape.

Pause to ponder, praise, and pray

If you're a parent, think back on the thoughts and feelings that flooded your heart when you held your little one(s) for the first time. Savor those memories as you relive those life-changing moments.

> "Before I formed you in the womb I knew you,
> before you were born I set you apart"
> (Jeremiah 1:5).

Pause to praise the Lord for His thoughts and plans, from before creation, relative to your child(ren). Thank Him for the height of His thoughts toward them and for the depth of His love.

Take a moment now to ask God to teach and guide your child(ren).

Show _____ your ways, Lord,
teach him/her your paths.
Guide him/her in Your truth and teach him/her,
for You are _____'s God and Savior,
and may his/her hope be in You all day long.

(Psalm 25:4–5)

CHAPTER 2

ADJUSTING
TO A NEW
"NORMAL"

"When one door closes another door opens;
but we so often look so long
and so regretfully upon the closed door,
that we do not see the ones which open for us."

ALEXANDER GRAHAM BELL

We returned home from the most recent hospital visit. It was late January, and I was eight months pregnant. This second pregnancy had gone by quickly; it coincided with all of Zach's surgeries of the past year, and I was so focused on Zach and all the health issues going on with him that I really didn't worry about this next baby. Trusting in God's plan for our family, I had chosen early on in the pregnancy to decline any prenatal testing that would have informed me whether or not the new baby also had Down syndrome. I made a decision not to let my mind be consumed with those nagging thoughts of "What if?" The one thing I knew for certain was that God is sovereign, that He knew what was best for our family, and that this baby too was His creation. In early March of that year our son Ben was born, healthy and beautiful. He was a blessing to our family and became a great little brother for Zach.

Ben quickly gained both pounds and skills. I borrowed a twin stroller from a friend and was often asked whether the boys were twins. Ben caught up with Zach in many areas, and the two learned things together—including the ability to walk. Ben was one year old and Zach was two-and-a-half. It was double everything: activities, strolling toddlers, food, and diapers. It was a busy stretch of life.

Zach was now enrolled in a class for two-year-olds through the intermediate school district. He attended two mornings a week, during which Ben and I enjoyed walks in the nearby mall. This was a pleasant one-on-one time for the two of us.

At ages three and four Zach attended a Pre-Primary Impaired (PPI) class. PPI was held outside our home school district, the class meeting in a school about 30 minutes from our home. A big yellow bus pulled into our driveway (actually it was a small bus, but when you're putting your three-year-old on it for a thirty-minute ride with and to strangers, it seemed big), right up to the garage. Zach and I went out, and I buckled him into the car seat already on the bus. It was a strange feeling that first day, but, as usual, Zach adapted just fine. He attended PPI four mornings a week for two years. I was beginning to learn that in these moments of transition and releasing it was me, the mom, who struggled and hesitated to let go; Zach was ready and willing. I also began to see how smart Zach really was. He was learning and growing even beyond the teacher's expectations.

This truth speaks to one of the difficulties I've discovered over the years. Expectations, generally, are too low, based on a stereotype or book knowledge rather than on experience or looking at the uniqueness of each individual. Wouldn't it be better if we set the bar high rather than thinking in terms of "can't" or "too hard"? Our children will live up to the expectations we and others set for them. If we set those expectations low, they'll live up to them, but the same may well apply to the anticipation of higher achievements. Let's not settle for stereotypes, not fail to stretch ourselves or our kids beyond what we may have seen or heard or been told they can accomplish. Instead, let's look at each child as an individual with unknown potential and see what he or she can do. Yes, the outcomes will vary, but overall these kids will surprise us!

Pause to ponder, praise, and pray

In what ways has your child, at whatever his/her current age, particularly surprised you in terms of surpassing expectations? If your son or daughter is a little older, when have you been amazed at his/her insight or wisdom?

Praise the Lord for the reality of Paul's observation in 1 Corinthians 7:7:

> "Each of you has your own gift from God;
> one has this gift, another has that."

Pray this verse with regard to God's purpose for your child(ren).

> Lord, raise up _____ for Your purposes,
> that You might show him/her Your power and that Your
> name might be proclaimed in all the earth.
> (Exodus 9:16)

CHAPTER 3

HE CAN
WRITE
HIS NAME

*"Simple pleasures like giant snowflakes
remind us that we are unique
in all of God's creation."*

ANONYMOUS

As Zach approached the age of five, our desire for him was to attend the elementary school near our home. This seemed like an obvious choice, as this would be the school where his siblings and the neighborhood kids would attend, and it was near our home. We really didn't even consider sending him elsewhere. I had grown up in this community and had also attended this school. This made the transition somewhat easier, as I knew several of the teachers and staff. However, I didn't know the principal or how he would feel about having Zach attend Hamilton Elementary. This was early in the history of inclusion in schools, 1990, and I understood that the openness of the building principal would be a key factor, not only in terms of getting Zach into the school but of his predicted success in that building.

I made an appointment to meet with the principal and talked with him about our strong desire to have Zach attend the same school as his younger siblings. Thankfully, he was very amenable to the idea, and Zach entered the developmental kindergarten class just after turning five years old. He attended half days, five days a week. We were blessed with a wonderful teacher, Mrs. Cross, who welcomed him into her class and treated him like any other DK kid—exactly what Zach needed—and exactly what I needed too! As I look back on this, I can trace so clearly how God had gone before us to prepare the way for Zach. God knew the best plan, and He opened up doors of opportunity for Zach to attend Hamilton Elementary. This was the first time these doors had been opened to a child with Down syndrome child in our district.

I'll always remember our first parent-teacher conference in November of that year. Mrs. Cross showed us all of Zach's work, the shapes he had drawn and the letters he'd learned. Next she showed us papers demonstrating that he had learned to write his name. This was both amazing and intensely fulfilling for me. My little boy was doing what the other kids were doing. This was just the confirmation Rick and I needed that we had made the right decision in sending our son to Hamilton Elementary.

Around that same time I read an article in our local newspaper about a group called Moms in Touch. This ministry, Moms In Prayer International, formerly Moms In Touch, impacts children and schools worldwide for Christ by gathering mothers to pray. Women meet for one hour each week to pray for their kids and their school. The article offered information about a group that had recently started in Hamilton. I was intrigued and knew immediately that this was an opportunity I needed to check into.

A few weeks later I connected with and decided to join this small group of moms who met weekly to pray for Hamilton Elementary and their children who attended there. I showed up the first time not knowing what to expect. *Really, pray for an entire hour? How is that possible?* Still, I knew I had to set aside my fears and go.

As it turned out, praying for that hour with those other moms was like nothing I had experienced before. It was a little intimidating at first, but also wonderful and emotional. *Pass the tissues, please!* I became a regular attendee, and the experience changed me forever. I learned for the first time how to pray aloud, and I prayed Scripture verses over Zach. Other moms, who didn't even know my son, prayed with me on his behalf. I made friends, relationships blossomed, and I still have a connection with many of those precious women today, 20 years later. Prayer, I began to realize, was one of the keys to Zach's success. It astounded me that I could pray with other moms for all of our children and that they seemed to know instinctively just how to intercede for my little one they had never even met. Oh, how God loves to hear moms pouring out their hearts to Him for the lives of their children. "Arise, cry out in the night, as the watches of the night begin; pour out your heart like water in the presence of the Lord. Lift up your hands to him for the lives of your children" (Lamentations 2:19).

This hour of my week, this single hour I spend at Moms in Prayer, this seemingly simple act of praying together with other women has, I believe, been one of the best things I've ever done—and continue to do to this day. For more than 20 years the Moms in Prayer hour has been one of my favorite hours of each week. If you would like more information about Moms in Prayer International, I invite you to check out their website at www.momsinprayer.org.

Pause to ponder, praise, and pray

To what extent and in what ways have you incorporated prayer into your parenting? What differences have your prayers made? Is there one particular answered prayer that stands out for you?

Praise God for the gift of prayer and God's promise in Philippians 4:6–7:

> "Do not be anxious about anything, but in every
> situation, by prayer and petition, with thanksgiving,
> present your requests to God. And the peace of God,
> which transcends all understanding, will guard your
> hearts and your minds in Christ Jesus."

Pray that your child(ren) may know the amazing, unconditional love of God.

> May _____ know that You are his/her God,
> who takes hold of his/her right hand
> and says to him/her, "Do not fear;
> I will help you."
> (Isaiah 41:13)

CHAPTER 4

I'M NOT AN ANGEL, SO WHY DO I HAVE A HALO?

*"Sometimes adversity
is what you need to face
in order to become successful."*

ZIG ZIGLAR

Zach has had some significant health issues to deal with his entire life. At around age eight he began experiencing a swollen knee. This continued, and the swelling seemed to move to other joints. Eventually we received a diagnosis of juvenile rheumatoid arthritis (JRA). We tried different medications, and for the most part this disease did not hinder Zach's ability to function. When he was eleven, however, he began experiencing pain in his neck. (Thankfully, *he* wasn't a "pain in the neck!") We wondered whether this might be a new manifestation of the JRA, and flexion-extension X-rays were ordered, as is often done to check kids with Down syndrome for atlanto-axial instability.

The results of these tests were not what we had been expecting. They showed instability between his C-1 and C-2 vertebrae, likely indicating surgery to fuse the two together. Another orthopedic surgeon to whom we went for a second opinion con-

curred with the diagnosis, sending us down a path that year
we never expected or wanted to take. We began to prepare for
a C-1 / C-2 fusion surgery, which would require grafting bone
from Zach's hip to place between the C-1 and C-2 vertebrae.
This would require putting Zach in a halo device for 12 weeks—
which wasn't good news. Unprepared myself, I was at a loss as
to how to prepare our son for this. How could I possibly explain
that he would awaken with four large pins through his skull
and wearing this cumbersome brace. I didn't know how we were
going to care for him, . . . but God did.

In June of that year we learned of a horrible auto accident
involving the daughter of our neighbors down the street, who
had broken her neck and been put in a halo. This occurred at
around the time we were learning of and preparing for Zach's
upcoming surgery, which was scheduled for early September.
One aspect of our preparations involved calling our neighbor,
Amber, and her family. We explained our situation and asked
whether we could come for a visit. I wanted to show Zach what
a halo looked like and hear from this family what we could do
to make this work for him. Our neighbors graciously invited us
into their home. Zach was quiet, not sure what was really going
on, while Amber and her mom, Judy, were helpful and kind,
giving me tips on how to care for Zach and make him comfortable. This firsthand knowledge from them helped tremendously.

The day arrived, and the surgery was successful. The doctors were pleased and, after about a week's stay in the hospital,
Zach was sent home. We had a hospital bed delivered to our home
to make sleeping more comfortable for him, and he slept in our
living room for the 12 weeks. The day we came home our neighbors arrived with smiles, balloons, candy, and encouragement
for Zach. We took a picture that evening of Amber and Zach,
both in their halos—Zach with 12 weeks to go and Amber with
only one day remaining. How amazing that their joint experience

coincided for that one day. A coincidence? I don't think so. I believe it was God, using extremely difficult circumstances for both families for His—and our—good and for His glory.

As the weeks went by this family provided much encouragement in the form of visits, food, and fun cards. They also gave us their special "halo shampoo bowl," a unique device that made it easy for us to wash Zach's hair right in the middle of the living room. Further "gifts" from them included tips and tricks on changing the fleece from the inside of the halo vest. All of this helped tremendously, and we will forever be thankful for the love and support these neighbors, just emerging themselves from a life-changing and traumatic event, so willingly provided.

Every day through this halo event we could see God at work—through people showing up at our door with Zach's favorite movies to basketsful of fun gifts and toys from ladies at our church. The favorite item in one basket was a large stuffed animal, a chocolate lab. The woman who had purchased this dog for Zach had no idea our family had a real chocolate lab—Zach's dog. She told me that when she was in the store looking for something for Zach God had led her to this particular gift. How amazed and thankful I was at this seemingly minor demonstration of the way in which God cares about the smallest details of our lives. The God of the universe cares about a stuffed animal for a young boy. Now that is cool.

Zach adjusted well to living with a halo and relished being the center of attention, established there in the middle of our living room. He wasn't attending school at all that semester, based on our decision to give him ample time to heal and recover at home. His paraprofessional (educational aide) from school came a few days each week to tutor him, and he received a visit every Friday from a group of classmates from his sixth-grade classroom. The kids came for lunch, invariably including Zach's favorite chocolate cake, as well as for the visit with Zach.

Sometimes we entertained groups of girls, who were usually polite and well-mannered and whom Zach enjoyed seeing. At other times the visitors were boys. Those visits were entertaining as well, as they wrestled and made a variety of noises, laughing together at each one. Zach has always loved a good joke—especially if it involved some bathroom humor! We both looked forward to the visits, and the added benefit was that Zach was able to stay connected to his classroom and friends.

The 12 weeks passed relatively quickly, and in early December the halo came off. Originally the doctors had told us that in kids with Down syndrome this surgery is at times unsuccessful the first time. But to our relief they reported that the surgery had been a success and that they were pleased with the results. We knew, of course, that it was God who had fused together those vertebrae. We give Him all the credit.

Once again, while this was not an experience we would have chosen, in the midst of it all we could tangibly see and feel God's amazing love for us and for Zach.

Pause to ponder, praise, and pray

Looking back on your family life, when and in what ways have you benefitted from a gift you would never have chosen? Be specific, moving beyond the obvious gift of your child as a cherished family member.

Join once again with this praise from Ephesians 3:20–21:

> "Now to him who is able to do immeasurably
> more than all we ask or imagine, according to his
> power that is at work within us, to him be glory

in the church and in Christ Jesus throughout all
generations, for ever and ever! Amen."

Pray for God to strengthen and uphold your child(ren) when
difficulties come.

Lord, You are _____'s refuge and strength;
be his/her ever present help in trouble.
(Psalm 46:1)

CHAPTER 5

JUNIOR
HIGH

*"Faith sees the invisible,
believes the unbelievable,
and receives the impossible."*

CORRIE TEN BOOM

Our entire journey with Zach has been like a tapestry woven together with beautiful colored threads to create a striking and unexpected design. As Zach moved on toward the end of elementary school, his speech teacher began to mention to me that in junior high there was a teacher who was simply the best and that her life skills program would be exactly right for Zach. I wasn't so sure. Throughout Zach's elementary school years we were experiencing "inclusion," a term that was relatively new when Zach was born and had gained momentum in recent years. Inclusion is the philosophy that kids with special needs have the right to experience the same types of things in the classroom as the "regular" kids and should get the same chances at school. I believed in inclusion, but as I looked at the life skills classroom at the junior high I didn't see evidences of it. I saw separation from the regular classroom, and I wasn't sure this was right for Zach. From the little I knew about the program, it appeared to me to be too exclusive, clearly separating the "regular kids" from the "special ed" kids.

As God's perfect timing and plan would have it, at around this time I met a special person. My husband worked for a builder, and one of the homes he was working on was going to be included in our area's annual Parade of Homes. The local Down syndrome support group with which I was involved at that time decided to take tickets at that home as a fundraiser and awareness activity. On the evening we were taking our turn the homeowner came by, and I found out she was a special education teacher in a nearby high school. We chatted about Zach and his schooling at Hamilton. To my surprise we met again a year or two later: she was the new life skills teacher in Hamilton. She had accepted a job at the school and would now be Zach's teacher, starting in the seventh grade and continuing through the twelfth. God was already at work preparing the way for Zach.

Input from Carin Von Ins, Life Skills Teacher:

Zach's family was excited and nervous about Zach moving into junior high. They knew this was best for him, but leaving the security of elementary school, the teachers and staff there who knew him and cared so much for him, would be a difficult change. It was scary and a big transition for all of us. We did the preparation work. We had numerous meetings and a number of discussions to make this transition go smoothly for everyone. Zach was the only student in the entire school district with Down syndrome, and we knew that this transition was going to be unique and eye-opening for many within the hallways of our school. I was honored that the Aalderinks trusted me and put Zach in my program. The general educators had concerns and wondered What would this kid do? With whom would he eat lunch? What would he do for gym class? Would he remember his classes? These were the questions asked by the general education staff at the final meeting before Zach's arrival in the fall. As I heard the negative tones in others' voices, I stood my ground, but I also wondered whether this "transition" would work. I needed to convince the others, but I also knew I needed their support and understanding.

And back to Linda:

So the wonderful years of junior high began. It was a scary transition for me but, thankfully, not for Zach. Are you seeing a pattern here? I'm the one with issues, not Zach. Zach has always enjoyed school. I can't remember a day when he didn't want to get up and go. Now came the seventh grade, in a large and different building with new teachers and a new principal and lots of new kids to meet. None of which fazed our Zach. Thankfully, he didn't perceive the potential hazards in the road ahead. He liked school and transferred that attitude to the new situation, showing neither concern nor hesitation. He became part of the life skills class, which at that time was a mixture of kids from the seventh through the twelfth grades in this combined building.

In addition to the life skills class, he was enrolled in general education classes in science, geography, and physical education. Approximately six weeks into Zach's first semester of junior high I met with his team of regular education teachers, along with the life skills teacher. The regular ed teachers questioned "What is he learning?" and remarked, "This is too hard for him." I sensed that they were ready to throw in the towel, that our attempt to incorporate this particular special needs child into the junior high was simply not working or workable.

My heart sank. I understood their concern; after all, this was brand-new territory for them. There had never been a child with Down syndrome in this school before, and they were not special education teachers. Still, I wanted this to work and believed in my heart that it would. I asked them to give Zach more time, explaining that he typically takes time to warm up to new people and that beginning in a new school building with all new people was a huge transition for any child, but especially one with special needs. Carin, his life skills teacher, agreed and backed me up. These teachers agreed to give Zach a bit more time. I was thankful for their graciousness and willingness to continue. This was both an answer to prayer and a call for more prayer.

Not surprisingly for me, it didn't take much more time before Zach acclimated beautifully to his surroundings. As the teachers got to know Zach, they genuinely liked him and enjoyed having him in their classes. I'll be forever grateful to Carin, who kept encouraging the general education teachers by telling them, "Zach is learning more than you'll ever know. It isn't just about the academics; Zach is learning social behaviors, both good and bad." Carin watched this firsthand and had discussions with Zach about appropriate and inappropriate behaviors. She noted that his hormones were at grade level and gave him good direction on how to handle this emerging aspect of himself so he would treat others appropriately and respectfully. She taught him the meaning and implications of the word "independent." Carin and I joked in later years that maybe we made him a little too independent!

Pause to ponder, praise, and pray

In what ways is your special needs child on a par with other kids of similar age? How can you accentuate the positives of those commonalities you notice?

Take a moment to glorify God, not only for the incomparable victory over sin and death that is ours in Christ but also for those day-to-day victories that come our way:

"Thanks be to God! He gives us the victory
through our Lord Jesus Christ."
(1 Corinthians 15:57)

When you pray this verse for/over your sweet child(ren), know that you are praying for God's will for them. What could be better or more powerful than that?

May _____ know that God is able to bless him/her
adundantly, so that in all things at all times, having all
that _____ needs, he/she will abound in every good work.
(2 Corinthians 9:8)

CHAPTER 6

CHALLENGES OF HIGH SCHOOL

By Carin Von Ins, Life Skills Teacher

The next big step was high school. After two successful years in junior high, it was time once again to move on. This brought new challenges and new opportunities. It just never gets any easier! Our school district had just finished construction on a new high school building. Zach's class, the class of 2005, was to be the first freshman class to enter this beautiful new facility. So this was new territory not only for Zach but for his friends and classmates as well—and even for me!

Zach began the special education curriculum, which I had pre-taught him in the seventh and eighth grades. I was also looking for new social opportunities for him, knowing that this skill would be essential for Zach's success beyond the halls of HHS. Zach has always been interested in sports, and it seemed as though getting him involved with one of the high school teams would be a great fit. Zach loves football in particular, so I decided to pursue the avenue of getting him involved with the team.

Football at Hamilton is a sport steeped in tradition and success. On Friday nights in the fall each game is a community event. I'll never forget my first conversation with Chris Myers, our varsity football coach. He was a bit unsure about the idea of Zach standing on the sidelines of every home game. I reassured him that Zach would be fine and asked that we at least try this once; then we would talk before the next game. The rest, as they say, is history. Eleven years later I'm still waiting for Coach Myers to get back to me for our talk! Zach is a huge part of the Hawkeye football program, and I know he has inspired many along the way. The program, in turn, has taught Zach much. He's learned about working hard toward a goal and seeing how the hard work pays off in winning games. He's learned about pulling together as a team, team huddles, enthusiasm, and encouragement.

Zach has also learned to wash the team's uniforms. This began as one of the life skills he learned in my program. Every Monday after a football weekend, Zach would begin the task of washing the uniforms. Imagine with me grungy, sweaty football jerseys that had been fermenting all weekend long. Didn't bother Zach! He loved Hawkeye football and performed this duty with the utmost care. The team appreciated the clean uniforms, all neatly hung and ready for the next game. (The moms of the players appreciated Zach's efforts too.)

Another Hawkeye football tradition Zach began was the cookies. Every Friday was game day, and every Friday morning Zach baked cookies in our life skills class. He made cookies not only for the team but special cookies that he handed out to the coaches with "magic sprinkles" on them for good luck. Later in the day, usually during the lunch hour or between classes, Zach would stand near the end of the senior hallway, proudly holding his tray of cookies. These were for football players—and football players only! On a rare occasion Zach might let his younger brother, a soccer player, have a cookie. The football cookies became a great tradition, something Zach and the team looked forward to each week. This gave Zach another chance to interact with his teammates on a social level and feel even more a part of the group. He felt as though he belonged to the team and was making a contribution to its success.

Although Zach has learned much, I think he has taught many of the players more about life than about football. At the end of the season the football team always makes a highlight reel, including clips of all the games and documenting memorable moments of the season. During Zach's senior year the coaches put together a story on Zach that included voiceovers with pictures from the players and coaches talking about what it meant to have Zach on the team. This piece is truly special, and we've used it many times over as we've gone out into the community to share Zach's story. Here are just a few thoughts from the team, coaches, and even the principal about Zach's participation:

"Zach has taught us to love life and attack life with a positive attitude."

"Zach has taught us to live life to the fullest, be happy with who you are."

"Everyone brings different abilities to the table. Zach brings other things and personalities. That makes him cool."

"Zach has shown the football players a love of the game. It's not about just Xs and Os."

"I'm grateful to have Zach around. He kept you going when times were tough."

". . . inspired the whole community."

". . . made Hamilton a better place. It's nice to have Zach around."

These words have reminded all of us that it isn't always about what we have taught Zach but also about what Zach has taught us.

Although Zach has now graduated, he's still a part of the Hawkeye football tradition. He attends all the games, both home and away, rides the team bus, and enjoys his role on the sidelines as "Hamilton's biggest fan!" Zach has built relationships with the coaching staff. He is affectionately known as the "Little Cheezer" and refers to one of the coaches as the "Big Cheezer." The football fans enjoy watching Zach's enthusiastic antics on the sidelines. He loves an exciting game, and I believe Zach will be a part of the team for many years to come. There's no place Zach would rather be on a Friday night in the fall than on the sidelines of a Hawkeye football game.

Pause to ponder, praise, and pray

If you or any of your kids has been involved in sports or other extracurricular activities, have you experienced lessons in "humanity" (perhaps including empathy and consideration, as well as sportsmanship) to be a positive part of the take-away?

Another educator of long ago, the Teacher of Ecclesiastes, made his own observations about life, including this:

> "I have seen something else under the sun:
> The race is not to the swift or the battle so the
> strong, . . . but time and chance happen to them all."
> (Ecclesiastes 9:11)

Praise God that this disconcerted individual came at last to understand the bottom line and common denominator for all humans:

> "Now all has been heard; here is the conclusion
> of the matter: Fear God and keep his commandments,
> for this is the duty of all mankind."
> (Ecclesiastes 12:13)

The following would be a great verse to pray, both for your child(ren) and for yourself.

> Lord, You promise to keep in perfect peace
> those whose mind is steadfast,
> because he/she trusts in You.
> I pray that _____ will trust in You forever,
> for You are the Rock eternal.
> (Isaiah 26:3–4)

CHAPTER 7

WHO'S LEARNING AND WHO'S TEACHING HERE? WOODSHOP 101

*"We could never learn
to be brave and patient
if there were only joy
in the world."*

HELEN KELLER

Carin Von Ins, Life Skills Teacher:

Another eye-opening experience in which Zach left his footprints in the hallways of our high school was in our woodshop program. Prior to entering high school in grade nine, Zach's mom requested a woodshop book for a summer preview. Zach is a bright young man, and whenever we could pre-teach him something he would be fine. Pre-teaching would give Zach a good introduction into the class, so that when the real class began he would already have a base of knowledge about the subject at hand. I approached the woodshop instructor a few days before school ended for the summer and asked whether he had a book for me to use over the summer, informing him that he was going to have Zach and his paraprofessional in his class in the fall.

He replied without hesitation, "Zach Aalderink? Are you kidding me? He'll get hurt! How is he going to function in woodshop? He can hardly walk!" I was so appalled I couldn't even finish the conversation. How dare this teacher make this kind of pat judgment? He didn't even know Zach. I knew this was something I couldn't give up on, and I also knew that Zach's parents would want to press forward. So we did. It didn't come easily or quickly, but in the fall of Zach's freshman year he began the semester in the woodshop class.

Not surprising to me, it didn't take much time before Zach and the teacher began to form a relationship. By the time parent-teacher conferences arrived that fall, the teacher was talking with Zach's parents about ideas to use tools he had specifically purchased to make things easier for Zach. He was positive about Zach's progress and performance in the class, and Zach's parents were thankful for his change of heart. Woodshop ended up becoming one of Zach's all-time favorite classes, and he became one of the instructor's favorite students. He took woodshop for a two full years and made all kinds of great things: shelves, small tables, magazine racks, jewelry boxes. All are treasured by his family and serve as reminders to them of God's interest in Zach's life.

Back to Linda:

Three years later, when Zach was a senior, he received at the Senior Awards evening a special surprise from his woodshop teacher. This annual event is a special evening for the graduating students and their parents, at which students are honored for particular achievements. The woodshop teacher stepped on the stage to present his department award to a deserving student, announcing that he also had an extra award that evening. He began talking about Zach and the progress he had made in woodshop and then announced that Zach was going to receive a special award the teacher himself had crafted just for him.

Zach's name was called from the stage, and through the applause of his peers and their families our son made his way through the crowded auditorium to the stage to receive his award. We applauded along with the rest and were again astonished at how God can work in any situation. Zach had learned much about making things with wood and loved to use his hands to craft these items. And this initially skeptical teacher had learned the benefits and blessings of giving someone a chance. It isn't always about what things may seem on the outside; there's always so much both beneath and behind the scene. As a couple, Rick and I have nothing but respect and admiration for this woodshop teacher who on a personal level had come so far. We, as parents, along with his life skills teacher, learned not to give up and to continue pursuing our dreams for Zach.

Pause to ponder, praise, and pray

If your child is old enough to be involved with professionals in "the system," when have you seen a breakthrough in terms of someone's attitude toward or evaluation or acceptance of your child?

What has this turnaround meant to you?

If this hasn't yet happened, in what ways have you seen results based on advocating for your son or daughter?

Thank God today for His role in our every success in life:

> "As long as he sought the LORD, God gave him success."
> (2 Chronicles 26:5)

Praise Him too for the eternal value He places on our glorification of Himself—a priority each one of us can "master."

Ask your heavenly Father to equip your child(ren) for His service.

> Lord, equip _____ for works of service,
> so that the body of Christ may be built up.
> (Ephesians 4:12)

CHAPTER 8

SPECIAL
OLYMPICS

*"The only disability
in life is a bad attitude."*

SCOTT HAMILTON

Zach was about 14 years old when he decided to join a local Special Olympics basketball team. Along with our son, the team consisted of several other young men with special needs from our area. Each had different abilities, but together they coalesced and became a team. They practiced once a week for several weeks and then played some games against other Special Olympics teams from surrounding communities. Throughout the season, whenever Zach had a game, the event was included in our high school's regular morning announcements, just as sporting events for other teams were announced. And on the mornings after there was often an announcement about Zach's game, how many points he had scored and the like. This was a way of validating Zach as a member of a real team. In addition to making other students more aware, it also promoted a common bond of interest.

Because of these announcements and their interest in knowing what was going on with Zach's team, a group of kids showed up to cheer and support at one of Zach's games—in a community 45 minutes away. They arrived prepared with signs touting "GO ZACH!" and went so far as to sport T-shirts supporting Zach's team, the Blue Devils. Their gesture was beyond wonderful—immeasurably beyond anything I could have orchestrated or hoped for—and I was frankly astounded.

Nor was this a one-time affair. This support and encouragement occurred again and again, season after season. At a home game for Zach our high school's entire varsity basketball team, coaches and all, came to watch Zach play. Those boys, too, arrived equipped with a prominent "GO ZACH!" sign. Each had signed it and wrote a note to Zach to encourage him. Wow! The support was genuine and heartfelt. Only God could have orchestrated something this good.

The following day I bumped into one of the young men who had been in attendance at Zach's game. I thanked him for coming, to which he responded, "It meant as much to us as it did to Zach." Wow again! The attitude of these young men toward Zach was incredible. They didn't feel sorry for him or do these things because they felt coerced. They did them because that's what friends do for each other.

For all of Zach's life as I've prayed for him I have often prayed for friends. In reality, I think that I, at least initially, was just looking for kids to be kind to him. I didn't want him to be mistreated, teased, or taken advantage of. My prayers were small; I asked only what seemed doable and reasonable . . . to me. What I didn't fully comprehend was that the God to whom I was praying is a mighty God, a God whose power and ways are exponentially bigger and better than my own. My understated prayers were answered in ways immeasurably beyond what I could have hoped or imagined. God always has much bigger and better ideas than I do. Instead of just surrounding Zach with kids who were nice, decent, and friendly, He blessed him with amazing friends—real, true friends. Many of these buddies Zach made in high school still keep in touch with him, making it a point to get together with Zach when they're all in town.

The basketball season continued, and soon it was time for March Madness. Zach's Special Olympics team ended up qualifying for the state tournament. Our high school has a tradition of hanging up huge posters for students and teams involved in big events, and a poster was prominently displayed in the main hallway of our high school wishing Zach good luck at the state Special Olympics tournament. Many of the kids took the time to sign the poster and wish him luck in the big game. On Friday afternoon of tournament weekend, Zach needed to leave school early to catch his team bus. I arrived to pick him up and was waiting in the high school lobby. As I stood there, a small group of teachers and students began to assemble. I didn't understand at first what was going on but soon realized as the crowd grew larger that they were there for a send-off for Zach.

A few minutes later, with around 30 people gathered, Zach came walking down the hallway sporting a Burger King crown. The gathered group spotted him coming and put up their arms to form an archway tunnel for Zach to walk through. Upon seeing the tunnel Zach began to jog, a huge smile lighting up his face. Zach ran through the tunnel to cheers and high-fives, as all present wished him great success at his tournament. Zach relished the attention of the moment, and as I watched I was overwhelmed yet again by the goodness of God.

In fact, I couldn't hold back my tears. *God, Your plans are always way beyond my meager expectations.* When I looked over at his teacher who had walked down the hall with Zach, we joined hands and enjoyed our tears together. This was a moment I will forever remember. A child to whom our culture attributed little or no value was also a child who was loved and cherished by those who had come to know him. Therein lay the key: getting to know him. This was a child who not only enjoyed his life but added untold joy and value to the lives of others. This moment of celebration was certainly memorable for Zach, but I have no doubt everyone who took part will remember it too. I couldn't have planned or even imagined anything so grand. Only God could. He did, and He still does.

Pause to ponder, praise, and pray

What particular experiences stand out for you as affirmations of your child's infinite value in the eyes of God and others?

As you dwell on this amazing verse, glorify God for His incredible concern for you and for your child:

> "The Lord your God is with you,
> the Mighty Warrior who saves.
> He will take great delight in you;
> in his love he will no longer rebuke you,
> but will rejoice over you with singing."
> (Zephaniah 3:17)

Pause for a moment to pray this prayer of protection for/over your child(ren).

> But let _____ take refuge in you and be glad;
> let him/her ever sing for joy.
> Spread your protection over ____,
> that he/she who loves your name may rejoice in you.
> (Psalm 5:11)

CHAPTER 9

FAMILY—
BRO/SIS

*"There is no doubt that it is
around the family and the home
that all the greatest virtues,
the most dominating virtues
of human society, are created,
strengthened, and maintained."*

WINSTON CHURCHILL

It's a beautiful thing to see how God has molded and shaped our family through the gift of Zach. In the early years I did wonder whether having Zach for a brother would be a negative for our other two children. Whether they might get teased at school on his behalf. I wondered whether they would ever be embarrassed to publically acknowledge the sibling relationship. I now know that my fears were unfounded. Zach has been known and liked throughout his life, and Ben and Kassi have been proud of his achievements. They've enjoyed the uniqueness of our family and have had their own share of laughs and cries throughout this journey. I'll let them fill you in on a bit of the story from their perspectives.

The Question—Ben Aalderink:

Middle child syndrome. It's a common occurrence among children who find themselves sandwiched between an older and a younger sibling. No matter which way you slice it, you're always stuck in the middle. I had a bad case of it growing up, but my diagnosis was different from most.

Because my brother had Down syndrome, I tended to fill the "oldest child" role, many times without even realizing I was in it. Still being the literal the middle child, I didn't know quite where I fit. This really gave me a unique experience, but one that I wouldn't want to give up for anything; the only reason my unique role was even possible was that my brother is who he is.

Over the years I've been asked a number of questions regarding my brother; those questions have given me ample opportunity to evaluate who I actually am and want to become. Because of those questions, and in large part because of my brother, I've turned into the person I am today. I can think of a number of experiences I probably wouldn't have had if my brother had been "normal." I'm very thankful for each of those experiences, though, and wouldn't want to give them up for anything.

Of all the questions I can remember others asking me, there's only one I've really learned to hate. The question itself tells me that many people are ignorant of what it's like to have a sibling with Down syndrome, or they don't want to take the time to think of other things to ask me. The question: "What do you think your life would be like if your brother was 'normal'?"

This lack of sensitivity makes me mad just thinking about it. This life I live is normal for me. So why are you asking me? It's an absurd question to even ask, and yet people not only insist on asking it but expect a response. An equally ridiculous question, albeit very similar, was phrased something like "What do you think your life would be like if your brother hadn't had Down syndrome?" You wouldn't know how to answer that question either, so why should I answer you? My brother has Down syndrome; nothing is going to change that, and I wouldn't want it to change anyway. I love him just the way he is.

Not knowing how to answer these questions, I would avoid them as best I could, saying things like "I probably wouldn't care as much for people with special needs" or "I don't think there's a good answer to that question." Or I'd simply resort to my personal favorite: "I don't know."

Many times I did try to fumble through an answer but was never able to clearly explain myself, simply because this kind of question seemed strange to me. I didn't understand why people would even think about asking me questions like that. I've finally been able to come up with an answer I believe will satisfy those who ask "the Question"—an honest answer I myself truly believe.

I'll get around to that a little later. In the meantime, one thing I've learned from my experiences is that the journey is much more important than the destination. So now I'll take you on part of that journey, and maybe, just maybe, you'll catch a glimpse of my life.

Let me say right now that my life would look completely different if Zach hadn't had Down syndrome. Many of my passions stem from the experiences I've had with and because of him. Even my personality has been shaped by him. I've worked with a number of people with special needs, specifically others with Down syndrome, and one of the things I've come to realize is that they're among the most stubborn people you'll ever meet.

The closest example I can come up with is that of a coffee addict. We all know one—the person who seemingly can't function until he or she has downed at least three cups of coffee and stubbornly refuses to do anything without this caffeine fix. Yet even that example doesn't do justice to the kind of stubborn I'm talking about. When it comes right down to it, the coffee addicts can eventually move on if they don't have coffee. They'll do everything they can to get it, but if they can't they'll simply substitute another form of caffeine or forget it altogether. The kind of stubborn I'm talking about is more like someone who literally won't do anything until they've had their coffee. Nothing you say or do can convince them otherwise. There have been times when I've proven my brother wrong by showing him proof of my point, even in a way that he would understand, and he still wouldn't listen to me. He absolutely refuses to listen to reason and will hold to whatever he thinks is right, logical or not, right or wrong.

Even though this can be, understandably, very frustrating to live and deal with, this attitude has quite frankly taught me a great number of things. I've gained an almost unbelievable degree of patience and generally don't mind waiting for just about anything. Throughout the years I've learned that this has even helped me understand more deeply my own relationship with God. I'm generally the kind of person who doesn't enjoy doing nothing. I have a strange need to be doing something constantly; much of the time I don't even care what it is. Yet as I've gone through life I've learned the importance not only of being able to take time to myself but to spend time with God.

Even now as an adult I continue to see the importance of Zach's influence on my life. A couple of days ago my sister and I took Zach out for dinner and went mini-golfing afterward. He was so excited he literally couldn't wait to tell everyone about it; shortly after we made these plans one of his roommates came back (yes, *roommates*; more about his living arrangements to come later in this book), and it was all he could talk about; in that moment nothing else mattered. To my sister and me this seemed like such a trivial outing, but to him it meant the world. Which makes me wonder: what would life be like if every one of us lived like that? What if each of us lived for the isolated moment, cherishing the present, not worrying about the past or the future but simply getting excited about the little highlights in life? How would your life change? How would the world change? At times like this I'm so very grateful for my brother's influence in my life; it's given me a perspective I wouldn't give up even if you offered me the world.

Actually, one of the most influential episodes of my life came not from interaction with Zach himself but is still directly related to his story. I have volunteered at Camp Sunshine for more than seven years now; if my brother hadn't had Down syndrome there would have been very little chance I would have even volunteered in the first place. Still now, camp is the highlight of my summer, every summer. It's the one part of my summer I stubbornly refuse to give up. Camp Sunshine is designed specifically for people who have special needs or are developmentally disabled. It's also unique in the sense that each camper gets to spend one-on-one time with a single counselor throughout the time they're at camp.

Not only do you get to know that one person extremely well during the three-and-a-half days you spend with them, but you always learn something from them. I've gained an unbelievable degree of patience from working at camp, something that most people (especially in today's hectic culture) think is impossible to develop. Patience is essential if you have any desire to work with people with special needs; as I've indicated, they're some of the most stubborn people I've ever met. There have been many times, as I've mentioned, when I've had an airtight argument against my brother's assessment of a situation, and yet he insists on doing things his way. My experience has been that you tend to grow the most in those moments of frustration and weakness, many times in ways you don't recognize at the time and can't begin to describe afterward.

Camp has been an incredible experience, both for me and my brother. Not only do I get to see him come to a place that accepts him, disability and all, but I get to see and accept others like him as well. One of the most memorable moments I had at camp came during my third year there. The entire summer before camp I had kept telling Zach that I was going to be his counselor that year, and I had other people from the camp back up my claim. By the time camp rolled around, I had him convinced that I really was going to be his counselor—which bummed him out. He didn't want *me* as a counselor. He got to spend time with me all year. He made it clear that he'd rather have one of his friends be his counselor—or, better yet, have a *girl* counselor. Instead, he was getting stuck with me.

On the opening day of camp I saw my mom and brother in line getting ready to check in. I made my way over to them and asked Zach if he was ready to spend the week with me. Not really answering, he gave me a dejected glance before looking away. At that point one of my brother's best friends, a counselor named Nate, came up to him and asked whether Zach would help him find his camper. Nate pulled out the nametag of his camper; upon reading it, Zach recognized *his* name, looked up at me, and, with the biggest grin I've ever seen on anyone's face, said one word to me: "*HA!*" Words could never have expressed the joy that came from him in that moment; his entire world had been changed in an instant. Now he really had something to look forward to that week: spending it all with his best friend.

I probably don't have to tell you that week turned out to be one of his favorites of all time. He loved every single minute of camp that year and wouldn't let me hear the end of it. Again, it's in moments like this that I'm thankful I have someone like him in my life. I've really learned to appreciate life and all the blessings that are mine, especially those that have come because of my brother.

I realize that the few stories I've told here cover only a small piece of my experiences and the lessons I've learned from

Zach, but they all boil down to the way I now respond when someone asks me *the* Question. Now, when someone asks me what I think my life would have been like if my brother had been "normal," I simply say, "That's a bad question to ask. My brother is normal to me, so I can't imagine life any other way." My brother is just like any other brother out there, and I love him because of that. Nearly everyone who has a brother would say that, but at the same time they would also say their brother isn't perfect either. I know Zach is far from perfect, but he's my brother all the same, and to me that's normal. He just happens to have Down syndrome. And I'm okay with that.

This *Is* Normal—Kassi Aalderink:

A lot of people wonder what it's like to be in a family with someone who has a disability. They wonder how my life is different from theirs. Or how I feel about not being a part of a "normal" family. The only answer I can give you is that this is normal for me. With Zach being my oldest brother, I've never known anything different. Honestly, I can't imagine life without him. I can't even fathom the thought of living without him, or living life in a "normal" family. To me, any other way of living would be strange. Is it difficult and frustrating at times? Absolutely. Does it test my patience? No doubt. But is it worth it? No question. It's absolutely worth it. Zach is such a unique, special guy. And he's always good for a laugh.

I swam in high school, and I don't know whether Zach ever went to even one of my meets throughout my four years. He didn't want anything to do with swimming. But one day I brought home a Detroit Lions swim cap with Jason Hanson's name on it, and he put that cap right on his head and wore it proudly. It's all in the perspective for Zach. He may not like swimming, but he loved that swim cap once he saw it had to do with the Lions!

People with Down syndrome, or just people with disabilities in general, teach us so much about life. I'm a counselor at Camp Sunshine, and this past year I had a camper with Down syndrome. It was interesting to see the similarities and differences between her and Zach. Either way Zach helped me prepare for her—and anyone else with a special need, for that matter—as my camper.

The first day at camp I had to tell my camper I was going to be gone the next night for a couple of hours because I had to go to a wedding. She seemed fine with this, and we moved on with the rest of our night. However, during the night's activities, without warning she broke into tears. I didn't know what was going on or why she was crying so I pulled her aside and talked to her. Eventually I found that she didn't want me to leave her the next day to go to the wedding. I was amazed. I had known this girl for not even nine hours, and she had already formed so strong an attachment to me that she was crying over the prospect of my leaving the next night for a couple of hours to attend a wedding.

These people are special. We need them. In so many cases *they* are the teachers in life, and we're the ones who learn from them. Without them so many lessons about life would go unlearned. I can't imagine a life without Zach, or someone else like him. I'm proud to be known, almost everywhere I go, as "Zach's little sister."

Linda again (of Grandpa and Grandma):

Grandparents are special people. Although I'm not yet a grandma, it seems like a great job. As I mentioned earlier, I believe the feelings and emotions of having a child with special needs in the family can be somewhat magnified for the grandparents. But the joys can be extra sweet too. In the case of my parents (Norman and Norma, with delightful names that nearly match, is it any wonder they have been married over 60 years?), while I concede that the initial hurt and disappointment were deep, I can unequivocally assert that the fun, the joy, and the bond they have created is something beyond what I believe they anticipated. Grandpa and Grandma adore all their grandchildren. They're the kind of grandparents who faithfully attend little league and pee wee soccer games, choir concerts, plays, high school sporting events, dance recitals, and graduations. They take the kids camping, both on overnight outings and to special places that are new and fun for them. They have enjoyed this with each of their grandchildren.

As Zach grew I could see an especially tight bond developing between him and Grandpa. Zach always wanted to be near Grandpa, and Grandpa always obliged. When it was time to sit for a meal, Zach wouldn't sit down until he knew where Grandpa was sitting. When the family gathered in the living room, Zach was always at Grandpa's side. My dad gave Zach rides on the tractor and behind the tractor in a wagon or sled, depending on the season. Grandpa taught Zach how to play pool, putt a golf ball, and drive a golf cart. And Zach in turn taught Grandpa to use Facebook, his camera, and his cell phone.

Grandpa doesn't have any special training in dealing with a special needs child. In fact, back when he was in school children with Down syndrome were rarely seen in public; they were often sent away to institutions to be raised by professionals. But what my dad did know was how to love. He wasn't intimidated by the label or diagnosis and didn't care about the delayed or sometimes almost indecipherable speech. Grandpa simply looked at Zach and saw an adorable and cherished little grandson. He treated Zach the same he did the other grandchildren, with love and respect, and Zach took to Grandpa like a bee to honey. Through all these years Zach has had a wonderful connection with Grandpa. Grandpa is his buddy. Always was. Always will be. This has been a treasured relationship for both Grandpa and Grandma, and the memories made will last forever.

Pause to ponder, praise, and pray

How have your family dynamics been positively affected by the presence of the special-needs child in your midst? In what ways has that presence made you a better person?

We praise You in awe and wonder at the intricate workings of God in the life of each individual person from conception forward:

> "My frame was not hidden from you
> when I was made in the secret place,
> when I was woven together in the depths of the earth.
> Your eyes saw my unformed body;
> all the days ordained for me were written in your book
> before one of them came to be.
> How precious to me are your thoughts, God!
> How vast is the sum of them!"
> (Psalm 139:15–17)

Take a moment to pray this verse for/over each of your children and their family relationships.

> May the God who gives endurance and encouragement
> give _____ (all names) the same attitude of mind toward
> each other that Christ Jesus had, so that with one mind
> and one voice _____ (all names) may glorify the God
> and Father of our Lord Jesus Christ.
> (Romans 15:5–6)

CHAPTER 10

REAL, TRUE
FRIENDS

"The language of friendship
is not a word, but meanings."

HENRY DAVID THOREAU

As I've indicated earlier, one of the prayers I offered often for Zach was for friendship. I think that in the beginning, when Zach was just beginning in elementary school, I was thinking of friendship as another child having him over to play after school, or perhaps inviting him to a birthday party. My expectation was probably so low that I mostly wanted other children to be kind—or at least civil—to him, to treat him with a measure of respect.

Children with Down syndrome can't hide who they are. Their physical features given to them by the extra chromosome are usually obvious. Thankfully, Zach didn't see himself as "different" or unlike the other kids. He was just a little boy going to school and desiring a friend to play with at recess, just like everybody else.

As he went through early elementary school, we found that a few boys really were becoming friends to Zach. They would include him in an occasional birthday party or invite him over to play. It didn't happen frequently, but it did happen, and for that I was thankful. They were nice boys, and we knew their families; relationships were being built. I began to hope that having a real friend was indeed a possibility.

As Zach moved into the junior high years and then on to high school, his "home base" for all six of those years was Carin's life skills classroom. This wasn't a "special ed" room where kids with special needs were kept separate or set aside from everyone else. It was an inviting place. There was always some kind of yummy food being prepared and an open invitation for the "regular" kids to come in and talk with the special needs students. It was appealing and fun, a place where kids could hang out and get to know one another.

During the high school years in our brand-new facility, this proved to be a wonderful environment for Zach, who got to know some of the kids, mostly upperclassmen to start. Friends made high school a wonderful experience for Zach. The following excerpts, written by Zach's friends, provide a glimpse into the hearts of these young people and the impact on them of their friendship with Zach.

Joel Kleinheksel:

I remember meeting Zach in first grade at elementary school. He was in my class with the same teacher as the rest of us. I didn't think he was different. For all I knew he was normal: learning how to read and write and doing simple math just as I was. We'd play on the playground together, and soon we were inviting each other over to play at our houses after school. I didn't know what Down syndrome was then, and it didn't matter; he was my friend!

I was happy to have Zach as a friend. I loved it when Zach would call my mom to see if we could "hang out" sometime, either at his house or mine. He always wanted to beat me at his favorite video game, and, of course, he always did! He'd invite me to go tubing on the lake with his family and thought it was great when I'd get thrown off. I'd take him for rides on a sled pulled behind my snowmobile in the cold winters of Michigan. I would be freezing cold, but he just wanted to keep going. I think he was having so much fun just living and enjoying life with a friend that the little things didn't matter as much.

Zach has taught me a lot about my own life. We often get too caught up in the busyness of our lives, our jobs, and all the trivial things that seem to run us. We don't like it when life doesn't go our way; we think we need to have everything planned out so we can be in control. I once came home from work worrying about all I needed to do the next day at the office, only to log on to my computer and read something Zach had written along the lines of loving his job and being happy to be able to work. I thought, "Why can't I have that kind of joy in all aspects of my own life? I can!" Since then I've been constantly reminding myself that God has given me each day and that I should be joyful in it.

I'm a truly blessed person to have Zach in my life, and I know he has shaped hundreds of people's lives in addition to mine. I think back to when I met Zach. He was somewhat quiet and didn't have many people who understood him. But Zach proved to me and to many other people that we could be different in some ways and still be great friends. Then I think back to our senior year of high school, when everybody in the entire school knew Zach and wanted to be his friend. There's no question that he blessed and taught something to all those people along the way—something about themselves, even if he didn't know it.

I often think about what "normal" is, but I don't think the word can be defined; everybody has his or her own "normal." For Zach, and those who are a part of his life, he's normal. He's a fully capable man who experiences pure joy. He loves to be a part of peoples' lives and blesses all of us in doing so.

I thank God for my friendship with Zach, and I pray that God will bless those unborn children with Down syndrome that they may be able to grow up and show God's love, grace, and joy to many people, just as Zach has done.

Alyssa Cooper Homkes:

Zach has been my friend since day one. He being eight months my elder and living a driveway away, we naturally grew up together. Many of my earliest childhood memories include Zach, from waiting in line at the bus stop for our first day of school to field trips and summer breaks in the neighborhood. I always knew Zach was different from me, but that never bothered me. He still enjoyed the same things I did—riding a bike, jumping on the trampoline, playing in the tree house.

One of my most memorable moments involving Zach revolved around the movie *George of the Jungle*. It quickly became his favorite movie, and he was never afraid to let everyone feel as though they were a part of it. I still smile thinking of him singing the theme song while beating his chest as George does in the movie: "George, George, George of the jungle . . . watch out for that tree." It was very entertaining, and he lit up when friends watched him reenact the movie he so greatly loved. Just as all elementary boys developed crushes on girls, so did Zach. In the movie George's girlfriend is Ursula, so naturally I was lucky enough to be one of Zach's chosen Ursulas.

Early on in my life I developed a strong sense of responsibility for Zach—probably through a combination of my being his Ursula and the fact that Zach was my first friend. I was the eyes and ears for his family, reporting on how Zach was doing in school, what was going on at recess, and who was sitting by Zach at lunch. I always took great pride in watching out for him. He was my buddy, and no one would get away with teasing him on my watch. I was never ashamed of him. I was the "big" younger sister, and I took my job seriously.

It didn't take long for Zach to acclimate to life at Hamilton Elementary, and later to both junior high and high school. Before I knew it we both were making new friends. While at one point we always had to play the same activity at recess, we soon were comfortable doing separate things. I remember always having to check on him from afar, but Zach's personality won him so many friends that my protection became unnecessary. His Facebook friends' list speaks for itself. Zach is a popular guy whom people love to be around. He will always make you laugh. Zach likes to talk to everyone and isn't ashamed of who he is—I still admire him for this more than anything else. Although I'll always feel like I need to watch out for and protect Zach, the truth is that he doesn't need it. He has become a great, independent man. I still keep in touch with my favorite neighbor boy—and nothing will ever change that.

Nate Vande Guchte:

It was a cool autumn day, one of those brisk days where you could almost smell the change in season, as winter was on the horizon. There are many memories of that day that remain crystal clear, despite the other details that are muddled. I remember exactly what Zach was wearing but nothing about what I was wearing. I have no recollection about what grade we were in or much else of what happened at school that day. Our story starts where every young kid's story starts: the playground.

As I ran around the playground that day, a crowd began to build. As all kids do when something happens on the playground, I too had to see what all of the commotion was about. When I got to the slide I finally saw him. Wearing a signature Honolulu blue Detroit Lions coat with a stocking hat, he was perched comfortably at the top of the slide. The crowd had gathered because he was refusing to go down, resulting in an impediment and a growing backup. The situation escalated, with some students starting to push for their turn to go down the slide. Still, there he sat, refusing to budge. Some climbed over him, some squeezed past him, and others just decided to give up their turn. The end of recess was approaching, and there was no time to waste! Suddenly I found myself at the front of the line; it was at this point that Zach and I came face to face for the very first time. It was my turn to make the decision. Would I push by? Would I climb over? Or would I just back away? This decision had to be made in a split second, or I too would be part of the problem rather than the solution. Little did I know then that this simple, elementary decision would change the course of my life. It would determine my career choice, help to establish my convictions and priorities, and even help deepen my faith and trust in God.

With Zach still sitting at the top of the slide refusing to budge, I decided to take a somewhat different approach. Instead of climbing over, or around, I simply asked whether he wanted to go down together. I expected some sort of verbal response, but instead he just smiled. He didn't say no—or yes—and he certainly didn't move. So I asked again, and again I was greeted in response with a very contagious smile. Once again he didn't say no, didn't say yes, and didn't move. Patiently I asked him once more whether we could go down together. I remember explaining that he could go first or I could go first; it didn't matter to me as long as we went down together. He inched closer to the edge of the slide and motioned me closer, still without saying a word. Then he grabbed my feet and we both inched to the threshold of the slide. He slid his feet off the edge, and inch by inch we slowly made our joint descent.

This voyage down the slide was unlike any other I had ever had. Like most other kids, my goal was to get to the bottom as fast as I could. Whether it was forward, backward, lying down, or sitting up, I didn't care, as long as it was fast! This time was different, though. It was as though time slowed down as we inched our way down. I truly noticed things I had never taken the time to observe before. Instead of being so focused on getting to the bottom, I observed what the other kids around me were doing, saw the leaves falling from the trees, and felt the wind on my face. Most importantly, I happened to notice the smile on Zach's face as he turned around. You see, when you're in a race to get to the bottom of the slide, or through to the next day, or hour, or meeting, in your life, you just don't take the time to notice these things. You get so focused on yourself and what you're doing that you never detect the finer things. This was a lesson I learned from Zach early on in my elementary years, but it's something I still haven't forgotten. In my life Zach's slow and deliberate descent has served for me as a consistent reminder to slow down the pace of my life, to observe what's occurring around me.

Next thing I knew Zach's feet hit the ground, and we ground to a halt at the bottom of the slide. Almost simultaneously the bell rang, signaling the end of recess. Before we had time to exchange a word, he took off in the direction of his classroom. What happened next is one of the clearest pictures of Zach I have in my head to this day. Running away in his Honolulu blue Detroit Lions jacket, he suddenly turned around and just stopped. He turned in the direction of where I was standing, and it was as though time had stopped. That smile appeared yet again; he waved and then headed back toward his classroom. As he turned around, it hit me that there was something different about him. My mind flashed back to the top of the slide, where he hadn't answered my questions, and for the first time I noticed that he looked somehow different from me. Yet there was something contagious about him, something in him that sparked an interest in me. There was no time to figure it all out right then; recess was over, and it was time to return to the class.

The bell rang yet again, this time signaling a reality altogether different. There were no more recesses for play, classes were much harder, and students were no longer grouped strictly by age. This time the bell signaled the end of fourth hour, and most importantly that there were only two more hours left before the big Friday evening game! The years of recesses were long gone, and we were beginning our third year of high school. As we walked down the hall, my friends and I were proudly sporting our football jerseys. As we approached the end of the hallway, we encountered a smiling young man, just standing there holding out a plate of freshly baked chocolate chip cookies.

We became excited as we noticed that he was handing out the cookies only to football players! As I looked closer I noticed something familiar, not all that unexpected in a small high school of only 700 students. Yet at that instant it hit me for the first time. It was *him!* You know, that boy I hadn't seen again since that late autumn day on the playground in elementary school. Doubts crept into my head, though. Could this really be him? If he had attended the same school as me this entire time, how could I not have seen him regularly? How was it that I didn't I know his name by this point in our educational career?

As we approached he continued to hand out cookies, selectively, to some of the other football players ahead of us, each time getting a high five. His face would absolutely light up with each one. That was it, I suddenly realized; it was that smile I remembered. My mind flashed back to the playground on that day so long ago, to that irresistible smile—the same smile I saw now on this young man! I knew he would never remember me, as I hadn't seen or talked to him since that day in elementary school. I had never saw him again out on the playground, and we had never had a class together. So how or what could I do to confirm that this was the same guy? How would I go about introducing myself after all this time?

Standing next to him was one of his teachers, assisting with the cookie handout to make sure the transfers went smoothly (looking back, it occurs to me that she may have been watching to make sure he didn't just eat all the cookies instead of handing them out!). Taking her aside, I asked what his name was. She told me that it was Zach and that he was a special education student with Down syndrome. I told her that I recognized him from elementary school and wondered whether she could tell me more about him later in the day. My mind was suddenly diverted from its sole focus on getting through the next two hours of class, and preparing for that night's football game, to trying to figure out it was I hadn't seen Zach for nearly seven years. Hadn't I been paying attention? Had he always been at the same school I was? I couldn't help but think about what could have been, and about why God had brought him back into my life that afternoon. The following two hours of class came and went; now it was time to get some answers.

After the completion of sixth hour I headed straight back to the place where I had, for the first time, formally met Zach and his teacher earlier that day. This time I introduced myself to his teacher, Carin Von Ins. I never could have imagined how this simple introduction would change the remainder of my high school career. That afternoon Carin told me Zach's full story. She told me that Zach did in fact attend Hamilton Elementary but that he was technically a year behind me in school, which may have accounted for my not seeing him in some time.

She told me that he was serviced in the least restrictive environment, which involved inclusion in the general education setting. She went on to say that he had been serviced by the special education program throughout his educational career but that her intention was to help Zach get to know more individuals outside his special education classes. I told her that I would love to get to know Zach better after all these years and that I truly felt that God was calling him to be a part of my life. How else would we have been reconnected after seven years? I was instantly concerned, though. How do you rekindle, or start, a friendship after so long a time? What if he wanted nothing to do with me?

Through Carin's introduction, leadership, and mentoring, Zach and I have been able to develop a profound friendship. I began to spend considerable amounts of time with Zach in some of his special education classes. There were days where Zach wouldn't say a word to me. We would bake cookies, play games, build puzzles, draw pictures, cook meals, and occasionally do some laundry. He would occasionally flash a smile, or whisper a quick thought, but overall he remained very reserved and even removed from me. As we continued to spend more and more time together, though, both in and out of school, I continued to see his personality transform and develop into who God meant and desired Zach to be. Zach soon became more confident around other people and even began to get involved with extracurricular activities and other students. The worries I had at first were quickly erased as we spent more and more time together. This was only the beginning of Zach's transformation into one of our school's, and our community's, most recognizable faces!

As a three-sport athlete, I spent considerable time after school in practices and competitions. Day after day, week after week, and month after month would find me on or around the athletic fields and courts. One of the ways in which Zach's teachers and parents felt he could become more involved with the student body was to increase his interactions with the high school sports teams by becoming a manager for some of them. This experiment started with football, and the momentum built from there into the basketball and baseball seasons.

One of my most cherished memories involves my senior year of baseball. As an outfielder I had tried to make a play on a ball that had been driven in my direction. I misjudged the catch, however, missing the ball completely. A run was scored, and the error was on me. We finished out the inning and I jogged into the dugout, extremely frustrated by my mistake and lack of focus, I just couldn't move past it enough to get my mind back into the game.

When I finally got to the dugout I noticed another person dressed up in the full catcher's gear. I didn't think much about it at first, until I looked more closely. The next thing I heard was, "Natharia, you better watch out or I'll take you behind the dugout with all of this on!" Please keep in mind that I'm one of the most competitive people you'll ever meet, but when I heard Zach say that, dressed as he was from head to toe in our catcher's gear, I laughed so hard I literally cried. I cried like a baby. Thankfully, I wasn't the only one.

I can't tell you whether we won or lost that game, but I can relate that the lessons I learned that day remain with me. I was reminded in that unexpected moment of what things are truly most important in life. I was reminded about priorities and the importance of a positive attitude, reminded to be content with wherever I am in life, no matter what may be going on. These are just a couple of the literally hundreds of life lessons I've learned from Zach. My high school career came to an end that spring, as did the sports seasons that helped Zach and me strengthen and deepen our relational bond. After all that, I couldn't help but ask myself, what would come next? With me going off to college, how would we continue to be so close? Were our most memorable shared experiences behind us?

One of the most rewarding activities Zach inspired me to become involved with was becoming a counselor at Camp Sunshine, a camp with a one-on-one counselor to camper ratio for individuals with disabilities. This life-changing event occurs each year, and it's something that both Zach and I very much look forward to. Through my first three years in this mentoring role, I never had the privilege of being partnered with Zach. But on the night before my fourth Camp Sunshine experience, I received word that Zach and I would finally be paired together as a camper and counselor! I'll never forget the joy and excitement I felt when I found out. I was so excited to be able to spend this special week with Zach. Knowing how much Zach looked forward to this week as well, I was honored to be a part of the experience at his side.

That week was filled with dancing, swimming, singing, and a lot of laughing together. These are memories I'll forever cherish in my heart. Camp Sunshine is a place where Zach and I were never stared at, never judged, where both of us could just be ourselves. So often we let those around us define who we are and shape who we become. My experiences with Zach have taught me to be comfortable with who I am no matter what others may be saying or thinking. He has inspired me throughout our friendship to refrain from judging others despite the way things may appear, and he has encouraged me to be myself, no matter what may be going on in my life.

My freshman year of college came and went, and it was time to get serious about what I wanted to do with my life. I had always enjoyed working with people, so I easily narrowed the possibilities down to two career choices. One was to go pre-med in order to become a doctor, and the second involved becoming a special education teacher in order to more closely work with students and individuals with disabilities similar to Zach's. As I thought and prayed about this important decision, I couldn't help but follow the calling God had placed on my heart to become a special education teacher.

Looking back on this decision, I can't imagine doing anything else. This has been one the most rewarding and inspiring career choices I could ever have made. There are days when I question the decision, but I'm quickly reassured by the endless memories of what Zach and I have shared together and of the enduring relationship we've built. I can't imagine not having met Zach that day (my life without either of those two "chance" encounters with him so many years apart, actually), or what would have happened if Carin hadn't gone out of her way to help develop and mentor our friendship.

I'm at peace knowing that God placed Zach in my life to help make me the teacher and person I am today. As I teach, I always hope there's a little bit of Zach in the way I conduct myself. I hope I teach with that infectious smile he flashes, and that I share the enthusiasm for life and learning he has so deeply instilled in my heart. When I think back on the way this all happened, I ask myself how I was ever so fortunate as to receive such a clear vision for the future.

Over the past seven years I have personally witnessed Zach transform from an unusually quiet and reserved individual to a confident, outgoing, and enthusiastic young man. I've personally had the opportunity to witness this unpretentious young man quietly change lives, inspire others, and bring smiles to thousands of faces. Zach isn't just a big part of who I am; he has truly become a big part of the identity of the entire community of Hamilton. Zach's enticing smile and enthusiasm for life have threaded their way throughout an entire town. If you ever find yourself in the small town of Hamilton on a Friday night, you might just be able to witness this miraculous transformation firsthand. I do have to warn you, though: his smile is contagious and his enthusiasm for life overwhelming. You might just leave a different person from what you were before you met him.

I've been fortunate to share some of the best moments of my life with Zach. They span from a victorious, last-second high school basketball game to a heartbreaking, last-second loss in the high school state football playoffs. They range from his standing in my own wedding to the funerals of close friends and family members. They range from sharing in the joy of the births of my two children to the fierce competition between the Hawkeyes and the Dux.

Zach was one of the first to visit after my wife and I took our firstborn, a son, home from the hospital, and he's genuinely interested in how the kids are doing each time we talk. His role in my family, in fact, has a lot to do with who we are and what defines us. As a special education teacher herself, my wife too was taken by Zach's passion, excitement, and enthusiasm for life, and I was moved and gratified at how quickly and deeply a bond formed between the two of them. If I don't pick up my phone on the first ring, hers will be ringing within seconds.

Zach may not biologically be a part of our family, but the mark he has made on us is indescribable. Zach has taught me so much about my faith and trust in God, and Zach's presence in my life has molded and shaped me in so many different ways. So Zach, I just want to publically take a minute to say thanks for your part in making me the man I am today. Thank you for inspiring, motivating, and challenging me to be a better friend, husband, dad, teacher, and coach. You've made my life Immeasurably More.

Scott Kooiker:

Webster's defines a friend as "one attracted to another by affection or esteem." And friendship is defined as a "friendly feeling or disposition." But what the dictionary can't define is what my friendship with Zach is like and what it has meant to me.

Throughout my life I've met a lot of people who stand out in my memory. I remember the days I met various musical artists and professional sports players. I can distinctly remember times when I've gone to see various concerts, sporting events, national monuments, and traveled overseas. I don't, however, remember when I first met Zach. I believe our first encounter was sometime in junior high . From day one Zach was a friend, and I never viewed him in any other way.

Our friendship began in junior high but really began to flourish during our junior year of high school. I was playing on the varsity basketball team, and Zach was planted loyally on the bench for each game, acting as our team manager. I was able to spend much more time with him at this point in our lives and came to realize how great a person he really is. He loved his job. You could tell that from his face and actions. No matter the situation, we could depend on hearing his cheers and on his getting the crowd involved in ways that only he could. You know God created him special when he turns to the crowd, mustering one simple gesture, and inspires all those people to rise to their feet, cheering as one. We didn't have the greatest season, but that didn't matter to Zach. He was happy to be present and involved at each game.

The following year, while I was playing varsity football and basketball, Zach was on the sideline/courtside once again. Each school year, as he helped out with the football and basketball programs, he came to mean more and more to each player, each team, and the community as a whole. On game days he would greet each player and hand out homemade treats. During the football games Zach would at some point be running up and down the sideline, cheering—and inevitably getting the crowd involved at a higher level. Still today he remains a staple on the sideline. It isn't Hamilton football unless Zach is out there.

During our basketball season Zach was involved with his own season with Special Olympics. To return the favor of being our team manager and friend, we acted as cheerleaders for him. I still remember going to his games. What an incredible experience. What I take for granted each day with my God-given abilities makes me take a step back. When I watch someone work twice as hard as me to play with maybe half the abilities, it's purely incredible. Win or lose, each game was about Zach trying his hardest and having fun. Why can't that be how high school athletes play today?

One of my fondest memories of high school was the prom. We had plans of getting together a group to go with Zach, who, unfortunately, became ill and couldn't attend. So a couple of weeks later about 10 friends put on a "Re-prom" for Zach. We all dressed up, had dinner, and then spent the evening together. It was incredible to see how much he appreciated this. It didn't make a difference to him that it wasn't a "real" prom. What did matter was the fact that some of his best friends took the time to spend the evening with him.

High school graduation came in May of 2005. It's funny how everyone plans on staying as close as they were in high school but then within a matter of weeks the group starts drifting apart. Between work and college it can be all too easy to let friendships slip away. But Zach didn't let that happen for our friendship, nor for that of our other close friends. At least every few weeks Zach would take the initiative to get in touch with me and a few other friends. We would set up a date to get everyone together and go out for dinner. Regretfully, we didn't do this often enough, though, thankfully, Zach kept us in line. I could expect a text message or call from him saying, "So when's the next guys' night out?" Through the long college semesters and summers working, this kept my friendship with Zach, as well as with many other friends from high school, close. It was always a joy to drive to his house and pick him up and spend an evening with good friends.

Unfortunately with the current economy, jobs are few and far between. I was fortunate enough to take one in North Carolina. But this meant moving 900 miles away from friends and family. Thankfully, I have a great family and friends, and I can count on Zach asking continuously when I'll be back next. And immediately after I give him an answer, I know he'll ask, "So when can we have a guys' night out?" It brings a smile to my face every time. Living that far from home shows you who your real friends are. And I can truly say Zach is one of my best friends.

On a recent visit home I stopped by Zach's apartment, and we chatted for a while to catch up. He's been there for a number of years now, and it's inspiring to see how independent he is. As a joke, I asked him if he would be moving home since this fall both his siblings would be off at college. To this Zach replied without hesitation, "Nope, I love it here."

I can truly say that Zach is a great friend who has been a pleasure to know. I'm grateful to God for placing Zach in my life and am honored to be his friend. I don't think I can put onto paper the full impact Zach has had in my life. I hope these thoughts offer at least a little insight into what his friendship has meant to me.

Pause to ponder, praise, and pray

What relationship outside the family circle has meant the most to your child? What difference has this meant for both of you?

Did this closeness "happen on its own," or were you or someone else instrumental in fostering and encouraging it?

Thank and praise God for the reality of Proverbs 17:17 in your life and in the life of your child:

> "A friend loves at all times, and a brother is born
> for a time of adversity."

Hit the pause button here and pray for real, true friends for your child(ren).

> Two are better than one,
> because they have a good return for their labor:
> If _____ or the other falls down,
> he/she can help the other up.
> (Ecclesiastes 4:9–10)

Zach at age 2

Zach and Amber wearing their halos

Evening of Re-Prom

Celebrating after a Hamilton Hawkeye victory!

Celebrating high school graduation with two
of Zach's teachers: Jeanne Page (L), Kindergarten;
and Carin Von Ins, Life Skills.

Nate and Zach after the Camp Sunshine talent show

Zach, Ben, and Kassi loving Camp Sunshine!

Zach and Jenny after winning the championship
and cutting down the nets

Driving the golf cart for Grandpa
on Monday morning golf outings

Grandpa and Grandma (Norm and Norma) Kleinheksel

Roommates celebrating with Zach
on his 25th birthday with, of course, Elvis!

The Aalderink family

CHAPTER 11

CAMP
SUNSHINE

By Carin Von Ins

"Keep your face always
toward the sunshine—
and shadows will fall behind you."

WALT WHITMAN

As Zach progressed through high school, I began to look for community opportunities for him to be with other individuals "like himself." He was the only person in our school district at the time with Down syndrome, although I don't believe Zach himself ever really looked at himself as different. He was always treated with respect, and he viewed himself as a viable and active member of the student body. I've been involved with Camp Sunshine for over 25 years. It's a camp for persons with disabilities, where each camper gets his or her own counselor; all are loved and cared for, and campers and counselors have a wonderful time together. The camp is situated at a lovely campground on the shores of Lake Michigan, where the campers get to enjoy the beautiful, sandy beach; the pool; and tons of fun activities every day.

At one point Zach's family decided to pursue the possibility of sending him to camp. After a year or two of just visiting for a short while, Zach decided to attend a full, three-and-a-half day session at Camp Sunshine. Linda dropped him off, and although I know she trusted in our ability to care for Zach I could tell this wasn't easy. I could see that she was teary-eyed as she walked back to her car that day. She was completely trusting me that the camp experience was going to be beneficial for Zach. As it turned out, it definitely was!

Each year at camp we could visibly notice Zach coming out of his shell. The first year, during the dance held one evening, Zach had to be strongly encouraged to participate. He preferred to observe and told his parents later that dancing was "embarrassing." Eventually he did get more involved, and today, after spending several years in sessions at Camp Sunshine, Zach is completely acclimated and absolutely enthusiastic. He takes part in all the activities and spends months before camp thinking about what his contribution will be for the annual Talent Show.

The Camp Sunshine Talent Show is truly a special event. It's held under a large tent, with a stage, microphones, music, and a videographer filming every move. Before the campers (aka the stars of the show) even arrive, a crowd begins to gather. The seats fill even beyond the edges of the tent, and refreshments, including popcorn, are offered to enjoy while watching the show. After the campers and their counselors arrive, each camper gets his or her moment on stage. They receive a personal introduction and then perform.

Some campers display the same talent each year, while others vary their contribution. The range of offerings is wide, from poetry recitals to singing to drawing a picture to dancing to basketball moves to superman flying to mime . . . . Truly, the talents of the campers are wide-ranging and wonderful. This is a night that blesses the heart of anyone who is watching. There's high energy, emotion, laughter, compassion, and encouragement one of another. It sometimes gets so loud and crazy under the tent that you'd think a rock star were on stage. There's nothing else quite like this special evening. Zach's parents tell me it has become one of their favorite events of the entire year.

Zach isn't the only person who thrives on Camp Sunshine. His participation has impacted his siblings as well, and both Ben and Kassi are now counselors at camp. When Ben was sixteen I convinced him to give it a try for one session; if he didn't like it he didn't have to come back the following year. Ben's been back to camp every year since, doing both sessions each summer and loving it! Ben signed up to be a counselor at Camp Sunshine to help others. He has definitely been able to do that, but even more importantly, Camp Sunshine has changed Ben. If he could pick only one fun thing to do in a summer, he's told me it would be camp. For a college student to choose helping kids with special needs as his top summertime priority says a lot about Ben as a person, as well as about what he's learned.

Zach's sister, Kassi, is now also old enough to be a counselor at Camp Sunshine, and she too has also fallen in love with the campers and the loving, accepting environment. In the middle of winter, months after camp is over and months before it begins again, Kassi confesses that she longs for summer and Camp Sunshine. She truly misses the campers she has come to know and love. This speaks highly not only of Kassi as a person but also of the camp itself and the unique environment it provides. The experience is a win-win for all who attend. Many—probably most—of the campers would say that the few days they spend at Camp Sunshine comprise the best week of their entire year.

Pause to ponder, praise, and pray

What extracurricular activity has been most enjoyable and beneficial for your child? What lasting changes have you detected in him/her as a direct result of this experience?

Thank Him for opportunities to make a difference in the lives of others:

> "Therefore, as we have opportunity, l
> et us do good to all people, especially to those
> who belong to the family of believers."
> (Galatians 6:10)

Praise the Lord for the privileges of opportunity!

Take a moment to ask God for mutual love between your child(ren) and those with whom they are in meaningful relationships.

> Above all, let _____ and _____ love each other
> deeply, because love covers over a multitude of sins.
> (1 Peter 4:8)

CHAPTER 12

HAWKEYE
FOOTBALL

"Individual commitment to a group effort—
that is what makes a team work,
a company work, a society work,
a civilization work."

VINCE LOMBARDI

During Zach's junior year of high school, his teacher called and invited us to come to the football pep assembly being held that week for homecoming. We didn't know exactly what was going on, only that it involved Zach and football. As usual at a pep rally, the football team is announced, and the crowd—the entire assembled student body and faculty—gets fired up for the big game that evening. At this particular rally the head coach for the football team stepped up to the microphone and began talking about a person who was an important part of the team and had made significant contributions. I wish I had recorded everything; it was a wonderful, heartfelt tribute. As a special honor, this as yet unnamed person was to receive a varsity letter.

When he called Zach's name, Zach got up and walked confidently up to the podium, shook hands with the coach, and faced the applauding crowd. At that moment one and all rose to their feet. Zach, unfazed by the attention, loved every minute of it. For Rick and me, seated in the top row of the bleachers taking in all of this, it was a moment beyond our wildest dreams: the entire student body and faculty giving a standing ovation for our Zach! I cried. I laughed. I stood in awe yet again of how good God is. Once again, as in so many situations related to Zach's school experience, I couldn't have orchestrated this moment. In fact, I had nothing to do with it, nor did his teacher.

The coaches' hearts had been moved to honor Zach in this way, and the crowd responded in appreciation for who these individual students and faculty knew Zach to be. They weren't applauding because they felt sorry for him but because they believed and affirmed what the coach had said about Zach. So many had witnessed Zach's contributions to the team, seeing him in the hallways handing out cookies and caring for the team's uniforms. They acknowledged his efforts in a simple yet powerful way, and it made an impact on Zach . . . not to mention me.

Why, I wondered, do I continue to be amazed at how awesome God is? He created the universe and everything in it; surely He can care for my child! What continuously moves me, though, isn't that truth itself but the way He goes about it. God has ideas and ways that are infinitely better—not to mention bigger—than anything I could ever dream up. My job is just to trust and let go. Sounds easy, but if you're a parent reading this book you know all too well that this is definitely easier said than done.

The releasing of any of our children can be difficult—the first babysitter, the first overnight visit, kindergarten, bus rides, friends' homes, driving their own car, college, and marriage . . . . And the need to release your child with special needs becomes more difficult by a hundredfold! As we let Zach go the first time to stand on the sidelines of the football game, we wondered whether he would be ignored or whether anyone would talk to him or acknowledge his presence. Yet as I watched our son on the sidelines that first game and throughout the rest of the season, I saw teammate after teammate approach Zach, pat him on the shoulder, give him a high-five, or put an arm around him. Soon I saw players handing Zach their helmets to lift in the air as together the team sang "The Victors" after a win. I saw Zach becoming increasingly comfortable on the sidelines and then, incredibly and on his own initiative, beginning to get the crowd more involved in the game. He is now a permanent and much appreciated part of Hawkeye football!

This high school saga has become such a wonderful piece of Zach's life and story. For us as parents, it was hard to let go but so worthwhile when we did—and even now, as we continue to do so. Our willingness to relinquish our precious son allows God a chance to show us how absolutely trustworthy He is.

Thoughts on Zach's gifts to football and Hamilton High School
By Chris Myers, Varsity Football Coach,
Hamilton High School

Our mission as coaches here at Hamilton High School is to use football as a tool to motivate high school boys. We strive to dispel what Joe Ehrmann in his book *Season of Life* calls the "myth of being a man." The myth in our society is that "manhood" is measured by three things: (1) athletic ability, (2) material possessions, and (3) sexual conquest. These factors don't make a man. Being a man is really about being a good person . . . a responsible and unselfish servant to others, an individual who strives to be everything God wants for him.

I first meet Zach in the hallway of what is now Hamilton Middle School. At that time it was a junior/senior high school building. His paraprofessional, Loie VanderBok, and Zach were walking down the hall between classes, and we introduced ourselves. Zach was the first student with Down syndrome I had met at Hamilton. I wasn't the head football coach at the time, and little did I know then the extent to which Zach would influence Hamilton football.

I remember Zach's mom giving a presentation at our summer football camp. To this day it was one of the most important things our players have heard . . . .We need to do it again.

Carin Von Ins, Zach's life skills teacher, took the relationship to a new level. Soon our players were making their way into Zach's classroom on a regular basis. Nathan Vande Guchte, Matt Mokma, and Bobby Knight stand out in particular as good friends to Zach during his high school years. Some people may be cynical and question this use of the word *friendship*. But I can attest with certainty that the time these kids spent together and the friendships they formed weren't about charity. These were mutual relationships that bettered all involved. I can state with certainty that Zach helped generally "selfish" high school boys appreciate the gifts God had given them.

Zach has ridden the bus with us to our away football games for almost as long as I can remember. In fact, he and I always sit together in the front right seat. Usually after about a mile he falls asleep. When he awakens we tease each other about needing more sleep and working too hard.

I love seeing pictures after the fact of Zach's "whirling, stomping, and dancing" antics during the games. You can't fake that degree of enthusiasm. He's always with the team when we sing the fight song after a hard fought victory. I cried when he got his varsity letter . . . He was *so* happy!

For me Zach helps keep priorities in perspective. As a coach I can get caught up in the details of game plan preparation, strategy, and *winning*. For Zach it's all about having fun and living in the moment. Sports fans are generally a fickle bunch; they'll support you as long as the team is winning but often turn critical when times are tough. Zach reminds each of us coaches of why we're involved in this way. We're trying to prepare young boys to be better brothers, sons, friends, and fathers. In addition, I know that, whatever the outcome of a game or season, Zach's support will never waver. He is without doubt our #1, most loyal supporter and a great player in his own right.

Pause to ponder, praise, and pray

In what ways have your own standards for evaluation and valuation of others changed as a direct result of parenting a child with special needs?

Thinking further back to your high school days, if you had access at school to classmates with disabilities, how did you view them then?

Knowing what you do now, how might your reactions and actions have been different?

Praise God for the uniqueness and importance of everyone He created:

> "The head cannot say to the feet, 'I don't need you!'
> On the contrary, those parts of the body that seem to be weaker
> are indispensible, and the parts that we think
> are less honorable we treat with special honor."
> (1 Corinthians 12:21–23)

Pray this verse and seek God's wisdom for opportunities and relationships for your child(ren).

May wisdom enter ____'s heart,
and knowledge will be pleasant to his/her soul.
Discretion will protect _____,
and understanding will guard him/her.
(Proverbs 2:10–11)

CHAPTER 13

IT'S NOT THE GAME, IT'S THE GIRLS

"To love someone
means to see him
as God intended him."

FYODOR DOSTOEVSKY

As you well know by this point, early on in high school Zach began to express a desire to be involved with the basketball and football teams. He has always loved sports—especially the Detroit Lions and the Detroit Pistons. After becoming involved as the basketball manager for the boys' varsity team, he would sit with the guys, huddle with them, fill their cups with water, and cheer them on. He thoroughly enjoyed being a part of the team and close to the action. The coach was supportive, as were the players, who were also his classmates and friends.

Our high school, as any other, had cheerleaders along the sidelines during the game and also performing at time outs, quarter breaks, etc. Zach, being the team manager, sat alongside the team at the end of their bench, affording him a front-row vantage point from which to observe the cheerleaders in action.

One of our friends, the husband of a couple with whom we regularly attend sporting events, observed that, from his perspective, Zach was really just interested in the cheerleaders. His wife and I laughed this off as ridiculous. Zach wasn't interested in the cheerleaders. He loved the guys, being a part of the team, the basketball game, and the cheering fans.

At the end of the basketball season, one of Zach's assignments for his life skills class was to write a note to the coach and the team. The teacher asked Zach to write about one thing he liked about being the team manager and one thing he disliked about the job.

Zach completed the task, and the letter was delivered to the coach. Zach's letter was something to the effect of "the one thing I didn't like about being the manager was that in the locker room the guys smelled bad! The one thing I liked about being the manager was the cheerleaders!"

I had to admit that our friend was right after all. We all got a good laugh out of the story, and it again showed all of us, and especially me, just how "normal" Zach really is—not to mention honest. That's one of the qualities I admire most in my son: he speaks the truth. I always know where I stand with him. It was interesting to confirm again, and in a different area of Zach's life, that he really was like the other teenage boys with whom he shared the basketball bench. Teenage boys like girls. That's a fact. I'm thankful for friends who can often see qualities in our children that aren't obvious to us. And I'm thankful for a God who gives us much laughter on this journey.

Pause to ponder, praise, and pray

Part of the description of the "Proverbs 31" woman is her ability to laugh at the days to come. Presumably she did her share of laughing with relation to the past and present as well. What one treasured memory of your child never fails to make you laugh?

Thank the Lord for the opportunity to focus on the fun and enjoyable parts of life, knowing he's juggling the hard stuff on your behalf:

"Cast all your anxiety on him
because he cares for you"
(1 Peter 5:7)

Ask God today for a cheerful heart and much laughter in your household as you rear your child(ren) (or just appreciate them if that passage of life is behind you).

May _____ have a cheerful heart,
for that is good medicine.
(Proverbs 17:22)

CHAPTER 14

LITTLE HOUSE
ON THE PRAIRIE

By Carin Von Ins

"The only stupid thing about words
is the spelling of them."

LAURA INGALLS WILDER

High school was great, though not always smooth sailing for Zach. One day that stands in my memory forever is when we caught Zach using an inappropriate word—a *really* naughty word! The principal asked me what we should do. I assured him that Zach's parents would not allow him to speak this way at home and that they would want him disciplined just the way we would any other student. Zach's parents' philosophy had been from the beginning not to treat him preferentially. This issue was certainly not an exception.

So we called Zach into the office. I had become a good reader of his body language over the years, and it was screaming to me that he was guilty—and knew it! We frequently focus on socially acceptable behaviors. This was a classic situation in which Zach was conforming to what any other sixteen-year-old would do . . . denying the allegations against him. Although this response was neither appropriate nor acceptable, I was actually excited that Zach was conforming to peer ways.

When the principal and I confronted Zach, he denied everything—while hanging his head low. I continued to question him, asking where he had heard this language. His answer finally came: he'd heard these inappropriate words on the television show *Little House on the Prairie!* I watched this particular show growing up, and I certainly didn't remember this particular word being used. I also knew that Zach's parents wouldn't allow him to watch a program with this type of language. Actually, Zach picked up on many social cues; most were appropriate, though some were not. The "were nots" gave us something to work on with Zach, and they also made everyone realize the extent to which Zach really was a lot like the other sixteen- and seventeen-year-olds.

Pause to ponder, praise, and pray

Have you felt threatened when your special needs child mimicked the unacceptable behavior, language, or mannerisms of more knowledgeable and less vulnerable peers?

Has it occurred to you that this budding conformity, when properly channeled, may signal positive growth?

Praise God for the better conformity His Spirit works in the lives on Christ's own:

> "For those God foreknew he also predestined
> to be conformed to the image of his Son . . . .
> And those he predestined, he also called;
> those he called, he also justified;
> those he justified, he also glorified."
> (Romans 8:29–30)

Remember that these words apply to *all* the children loved by our inclusive God!

This is one of those verses that's good to commit to memory. I've used it often over the years for my kids. Pray it for/over your child(ren) right now:

"Lord, do not let any unwholesome talk
come out of _____'s mouth, but only what is helpful
for building others up according to their needs,
that it may benefit those who listen."
(Ephesians 4:29)

CHAPTER 15

NOT PROM,
BUT RE-PROM

"The best and most beautiful things
in the world cannot be seen or even touched—
they must be felt with the heart."

HELEN KELLER

To return to a sequence of incidents mentioned by one of Zach's high school friends in an earlier chapter, one of the special events of the year for most high school students is the prom. This evening provides a rare opportunity for students to look their best, dress in their finest, and enjoy making special memories together. As a senior, Zach decided to attend, an experience his dad and I had always hoped he could have. This was an exciting time: picking out a tuxedo, making plans for dinner, and getting pictures taken. But the evening before the big event Zach became ill. I knew this was a reaction to a medication he'd been taking, so I hoped with all my heart he would be feeling better the following day.

Unfortunately, that didn't happen. He continued to rest but just couldn't snap out of it. Late that afternoon I called one of the friends with whom Zach had been planning to attend and broke the news that Zach wouldn't be able to go. I knew

Zach was disappointed, and Rick and I were as well. I remember sitting outside that afternoon and having a good cry. This was his one chance, we believed, to be a part of such a special evening, and now he was going to miss it. We still hoped that maybe, just maybe, we'd be able to drive him out to the prom site later in the evening, just to be a part of the event for a short while. Unfortunately, that didn't happen either. At prom picture time we left Zach home and went to the home where Ben was meeting friends for pictures and then dinner before the prom. They asked about Zach, and we informed them what was going on. Ben called later from the prom, asking whether Zach would make it at all. Sadly, the answer was no.

Zach spent the evening with his dad, watching one of his favorite movies, *Star Wars*. At one point Rick said he saw a tear coursing down Zach's cheek as he lay on the couch. Talk about ripping your heart out! Our son was understandably sad about being unable to spend this special evening with his friends. This incident reinforced for me that although Zach might not always be able to verbalize his feelings, his emotions run as deep and can be as poignant as anyone else's. It isn't accurate to surmise that because a person doesn't share the same IQ as others he or she lacks feeling or understanding. Zach completely understood both the circumstances and the ramifications of missing this once-in-a-lifetime opportunity, but he didn't or couldn't articulate his response. The tear on his cheek was evidence enough.

Life goes on, for all of us, despite and after disappointments, and the day after the prom was Mother's Day. Family members were coming over, and I asked our boys to put on their tuxedos so I could get a picture of them together. Moms need to capture these moments in photographs, don't we? I was even able to get a picture of Zach and a couple of his equally dressed up friends, who came over to our house that day decked out specifically for this purpose. This gesture really touched our hearts.

Fast forward one week. We learned from our son Ben and his best friend, Ally, that Ally's family would be hosting a "re-prom." They had been so moved by Zach's misfortune that they had decided to recreate the evening in his honor. Was that a great idea, or what?

Zach, along with many others, received official invitations. On the evening of the re-prom, all the kids showed up at our home in advance for pictures. The guys were dressed in ties, dress shirts, and dress pants, and the girls wore their prom gowns. We were able to take wonderful pictures before they all trooped off to dinner, which Ally's parents hosted at their family home, cooking the kids a steak dinner. All involved enjoyed another evening together, and the girls had another event on which to wear their beautiful gowns.

Rick and I could hardly believe how wonderful this all was. This family we didn't know all that well at the time had gone to such trouble and expense for our Zach. This represented another one of those amazing God sightings—another tribute which, yet again, I could never have devised myself. Only God can move in the hearts of people to plan and follow through with something so selfless and wonderful. This family somehow "got" the sadness and disappointment we all felt when Zach couldn't attend the prom, and they acted on the basis of their empathy for Zach and even for us. They didn't just express their regret but acted on it in a big, impactful way. This was an evening we'll remember always. Thank you, Velderman family!

Pause to ponder, praise, and pray

When you think back on life with your child, what particular God sighting comes to mind for you? Why was it so meaningful? To your child? To you as mom/as parents?

Praise God for always being on our side:

> "What, then, shall we say in response to these things?
> If God is for us, who can be against us?
> He who did not spare his own Son,
> but gave him up for us all—how will he not also,
> along with him, graciously give us all things?"
> (Romans 8:31–32)

Ask God to allow your child(ren) and you to both experience and manifest all of the fruits of the Spirit.

> Lord Jesus, grant _____ the fruits of the Spirit—
> love, joy, peace, patience, kindness, goodness,
> faithfulness, gentleness and self-control.
> (Ephesians 5:22–23)

CHAPTER 16

DREAMS
REALLY CAN
COME TRUE—
HIGH SCHOOL
GRADUATION

*"The future belongs to those
who believe in the beauty
of their dreams."*

ELEANOR ROOSEVELT

Families love reasons to celebrate, and graduations in particular are special seasons of life. They swell a parent's heart with pride at the accomplishments of their child. Perhaps especially in Zach's case, Rick and I were amazed and humbled at all our son had learned and the challenges he had faced and overcome.

Then again, I realize, there are those parents for whom graduation is a day that couldn't come soon enough. For their children, school has been a struggle and a daily grind. Many days can go by leaving these parents to wonder whether their child will actually gain enough credits to graduate. For some families the suspense lasts almost until graduation day. For them there is relief, thankfulness that the formal education for their child is over and that they've made it, even if just barely.

Graduation day for Zach represented a "way out there" dream for me. In our son's younger years I had allowed myself to envision him strolling across the stage in a cap and gown. But as he grew there were many years during which I hardly dared entertain this dream. It was just too big, too grandiose, perhaps even completely audacious and out of reach. Early on, my goals hadn't evolved beyond getting him into the schools. By "in," I mean just enrolled and attending classes—"in the door" of the neighborhood school.

As I've indicated, when Zach began in our local public school, the concepts of "mainstreaming" and "inclusion" were relatively new. The majority of special needs kids still attended "special schools," segregated facilities reserved for kids with disabilities. As Zach progressed through elementary, junior high, and finally high school, my dream of him one day crossing that stage in a cap and gown along with his classmates began to seem more and more feasible.

Even allowing myself to imagine this moment never failed to elicit an emotional response in my heart. Each year in May I would attend our high school's graduation to witness the commencements of nieces, nephews, or friends' children. As I listened to the names being called and watched the graduates cross the stage one by one, shaking hands with administrators and being handed a diploma, tears would come to my eyes at the mere thought of Zach one day being in their number. How could I dare hope that a child with Down syndrome might be able to graduate? Recent as the dates may seem, this was still truly uncharted territory.

As one year succeeded another, though, we began to believe and then to realize that graduation was indeed going to happen. This was going to be a big deal—a young man with Down syndrome graduating from his hometown high school! I recognized that it had happened before, in other schools in other places, but this was a first for our community—and a momentous event for us as a family. Pride and gratitude filled our hearts. God had made a way when at times there had seemed to be no way.

The week prior to the graduation ceremony our family attended a baccalaureate service for his class, hosted by a local church. This would be the first time we would see our oldest in his cap and gown. With Zach all decked out in a black gown, with a gold band around his neck, graduation cap, and tassel, it was a day tailor made for picture taking. Rick and I acted like the parents of any other firstborn child, arriving early to snag "good seats." Zach would be coming down the aisle soon, and we weren't going to miss a step of his progression!

The music starting playing, and the processional began; there, soon enough, was our Zach. I learned that day how difficult it is to take pictures when your eyes are filled with tears. I remember wondering over and over again to myself "How could this be?" This child was actually graduating! Pride and joy threatened to burst our hearts. After the ceremony Zach enjoyed posing with all of his friends for pictures. We lingered for a long time, snapping shots that seemed to include everyone in his entire class. He particularly enjoyed getting in with groups of girls for this purpose. That day was spectacular, and it wasn't even graduation.

Before we knew it, though, the big day arrived. My emotions were running high, and I fully expected to be weeping throughout the ceremony, especially when Zach crossed the stage. After all, I'd been imagining this moment for years and had shed tears even as I'd visualized the event!

As he walked down the aisle, Zach's face was suffused with his characteristic, winning smile. He, too, was proud of his accomplishments, and this day he was sharing them with the many friends he had made along the way. As his name was read, and Zach crossed the stage to receive his "diploma," I was enveloped and overwhelmed by the goodness of God. But, surprisingly, I didn't cry. Looking back, I think I was completely at peace and incredibly thankful for all God had done in and through Zach.

The Lord had indeed both gone before us and been with us every step of this journey, and now we were coming to the conclusion of what might end up being the best years of our son's life. We didn't know what the future might hold but couldn't imagine it could get any better than this. We savored to the full this bittersweet moment and the celebration afterward, as we followed Zach around our high school cafeteria after the ceremony to take his picture yet again with every friend with whom he met up. To resort to extreme understatement, this was a memorable and fun day none of us will ever forget.

Pause to ponder, praise, and pray

What event in the life of your family related to your child stands out for you as momentous and unforgettable?

Can you recall what thoughts ran through your mind?

Was gratitude to God, as well as to other people instrumental in making this moment a reality, prominent among them?

Verbalize your praise in the words of 1 Chronicles 16:10–11, written to commemorate a special celebration in Israel's history:

> "Glory in his holy name;
> let the hearts of those who seek the LORD rejoice.
> Look to the LORD and his strength;
> seek his face always."

Pray for your child(ren) to see God's hand in their life.

May _____ remember the deeds of the Lord;
may he/she remember Your miracles long ago.
May _____ meditate on all Your works
and consider all Your mighty deeds.
(Psalm 77:11–12)

CHAPTER 17

LET'S PARTY
ALL NIGHT

> *"God cannot give us a happiness*
> *and peace apart from Himself,*
> *because it is not there.*
> *There is no such thing."*

C. S. LEWIS

In recent years it had become a tradition at our high school for parents to sponsor a celebration for the new graduates only. The purpose was to provide a safe environment for them to enjoy a party together after graduating. A committee of parents had met during the entire previous year to plan and raise funds for this event. Rick and I had been a part of this committee, so we also were able to chaperone the party. I was pleased about this arrangement, thinking it would be good if we were there for Zach if he needed anything. After all, the party didn't begin until 11 p.m. or end until 6 a.m. As his protective mom, I still had a lot to learn.

This was one of those times when Zach really surprised us. He's typically a kid who needs lots of sleep, as in ten to twelve hours a night. We didn't expect he would make it staying up all night, so we had a sleeping bag and pillow along for whenever he decided to crash.

The night went on, and as I sat in one of the food areas to chaperone my section of the building, Zach came to talk with me. It was probably around 2 a.m. I was expecting him to tell me he was tired and ready to sleep. Instead, he rolled up his sleeves to show me the temporary tattoos he had just gotten and began to tell me about what he was going to do next: miniature golfing. There was no slowing down this kid. He had a great night and was more chipper and alert than we were when morning rolled around. This had been a special night of spending time with friends, and he had enjoyed everything it had to offer—once again showing me how truly "normal" he is in many ways. I continued to be humbled by this amazing child of mine.

Pause to ponder, praise, and pray

The words of the Teacher in Ecclesiastes 12:1 may trouble those of us who parent kids with limited prospects:

> "Remember your Creator
> in the days of your youth,
> before the days of trouble come
> and the years approach when you will say,
> 'I find no pleasure in them.'"

If your child has completed fulfilling high school years, have you been concerned about a "letdown" characterized by a more humdrum adulthood?

Has a slower pace and lack of excitement materialized and become a significant issue? Or have you been pleasantly surprised by new vistas, opportunities, and highlights?

If you do find yourself troubled by the prospect of a less than fulfilling adulthood for your special needs child, allow the Spirit to direct your praise and petitions at this critical junction, taking comfort in His intercession and intervention on behalf of you and your child:

> "We do not know what to pray for, but the Spirit himself
> intercedes for us through wordless groans.
> And he who searches our hearts knows the mind of the Spirit,
> because the Spirit intercedes for God's people
> in accordance with the will of God."
> (Romans 8:26–27)

Ask God to grant you and your child(ren) peace in this journey as you together learn to trust in Him.

> May the God of hope fill _____ with all joy and peace
> as he/she trusts in him, so that _____ may overflow
> with hope by the power of the Holy Spirit.
> (Romans 15:13)

CHAPTER 18

THE BEST
DAY EVER

> *"God always gives His best*
> *to those who leave*
> *the choice with Him."*

JIM ELLIOTT

A dream come true deserves at least one party, right? We gave Zach a graduation open house around ten days after the big event. I gave Zach some of his name cards from the graduation announcement with the open house information printed on the back and told him he could pass them out to his friends at school to invite them to his open house. After the first day he came back and asked for more cards. I don't know how many he actually passed out, but I do know that he considers lots of people as his friends—and he invited them all!

God blessed us with a spectacular, picture-perfect early June day. The sun was shining and the temperature was warm. I had tables set up with pictures of Zach and special keepsakes he had received. In addition, there were tables filled with Zach's favorite foods and the cake he had selected for this day. Dear friends came and helped with the food and kitchen detail. As a family, we could now simply enjoy the day. *Oh, God, You are good!*

As the guests began to arrive, Zach stood in the driveway to greet each one personally. It was fun to see him shaking hands and hugging his guests. He had the opportunity to see lots of his friends, and we enjoyed a chance to reconnect with some teachers from his preschool and elementary years with whom we had kept in touch. Zach was putting into practice many of the things he had learned through the years: looking people in the eyes, shaking hands, and giving a proper greeting. There were guests coming and going for over three hours, and Zach spoke with them all! This day was all about Zach, and he embraced it, though it was also wonderful and special for our entire family. I know, as his mom, that this will be a memory I'll treasure always—a recollection of one of the best days ever!

Pause to ponder, praise, and pray

What memories do you cherish of your own "best day ever" with your child?

First Kings 8:66 refers to a totally unrelated celebration:

> "They blessed the king and then went away, joyful and
> glad in heart for all the good things the Lord had done
> for his servant David and his people Israel."
> (1 Kings 8:66)

Yet joy and gladness of heart for God's good gifts can have continuous currency in our lives—whether we're celebrating a momentous event or just thankfully living day to day.

Ask God to be with your child(ren) through their changing passages of life. As You have reminded us in Your Word, there is a time for everything, a season for every activity (Ecclesiastes 3:1). Even when _____'s season of festivity has run its course, help him/her to savor a fulfilling life in relationship with Yourself. Help us to remember that our "best years" with You are yet to come.

CHAPTER 19

TIMBER WOLF LAKE— YOUNG LIFE CAMP

*"The best thing about the future
is that it comes one day at a time."*

ABRAHAM LINCOLN

This year, sending Zach off to Timber Wolf Lake was a piece of cake. He knows the camp, has friends there, and was eager to go. Contrast that to two years earlier, when the opportunity for another camping experience presented itself through my conversation with a friend. Zach showed little to no interest, but he didn't say no. After discussions, questions, and some encouragement, Zach agreed to go. Our deal was that if he didn't like camp, he would call home after a few days and we would pick him up. On a hot, sunny Sunday afternoon, we met the Young Life group at a local church. We signed him in, met a couple of the leaders, and waited for departure.

When it was time for the van caravan to leave, Zach climbed into a vehicle packed with stuff and Capernaum campers, most of whom he had never laid eyes on before. Capernaum is Young Life's ministry to special needs kids. Zach was slightly familiar with one young man, Bradley. And we met a Young Life leader named Paul for the first time; his wife, Lyn, who would not be accompanying the campers, was the Young Life director. Meeting both of them put us as ease, assured that Zach would be well cared for at camp. Yet the experience would involve a whole week away from home. Zach had never been gone that long before, and he still wasn't looking too excited about the prospect. I felt that maybe we should abandon the whole idea, even at this late hour. *Had I pushed him into a place where he would be lonely, miserable, and homesick?*

As the van pulled away, we waved—well, actually, I waved and cried. As difficult as it was to let go, God had instilled in me a peace that we were doing the right thing and that this was a great opportunity for Zach. I continued to pray over this new adventure on which Zach was embarking.

The days passed, one, two, three . . . . I thought I certainly would have gotten a call from Zach by this time. Finally I could stand it no longer! I called Lyn, asking, "Have you heard anything at all?" No, she hadn't, but she was going up there on the following day and would specifically check how Zach was faring. Upon her return, the report was, "He's doing great and enjoying himself!" I was relieved but still wanted to see for myself. So Rick and I took a day and drove up to Lake City, both to see the camp and to say hello to Zach. Upon our arrival, Zach barely cared to give us the time of day. He was settled in, comfortable, and enjoying everything about this adventure. We drove home, thanking God for His amazing way of meeting our needs and answering our fears in such abundant ways.

Zach had accomplished a ropes course, a zip line, an obstacle course, and lots of walking and other activities through seven whole days. He had done things that week I had never imagined he would even attempt. As his mom, I learned another lesson about releasing one's child. As difficult as it may be, I needed to trust God. He'll go with all our kids, even when we can't. He is omnipresent: present in all places and at all times.

And He's omniscient, always seeing and orchestrating the big picture.

This one week at camp opened up other opportunities for Zach. He has continued to return to Timber Wolf Lake for several years now and has also taken advantage of the opportunity to spend a whole month there to serve as equipment manager for the entire summer session. This was a real test of his independence. And I'm thrilled to say he passed!

Pause to ponder, praise, and pray

Reflect on your first or most agonizing time of parting with your child. How did it feel to relinquish him/her to the care of another?

Did you derive peace and comfort from your knowledge of God's oversight and care?

> "When I was a child, I talked like a child, I thought
> like a child, I reasoned like a child. When I became
> a man, I put the ways of childhood behind me."
> (1 Corinthians 13:11)

These words may not be applicable, or completely applicable, for your child. Even so, pause now to glorify God for the developing independence you have seen/are seeing in his or her life.

Pray for many opportunities for your child(ren) in their future.

> Lord, You have assigned _____ his/her portion and cup;
> You have made his/her lot secure.
> The boundary lines have fallen for _____ in pleasant places;
> surely, _____ has a delightful inheritance. (Psalm 16:5–6)

CHAPTER 20

I LOVE
MY LIFE

*"I found that if you love life,
life will love you back."*

ARTHUR RUBINSTEIN

After months of thinking and praying about it, the time had come. The packet from Friendship House had arrived. Friendship House is a recently opened housing development on the campus of Western Theological Seminary in Holland, Michigan. It provides a unique housing option for singles training for ministry, giving them the opportunity to live in community with high-functioning, cognitively impaired adults. Friendship House is the only one of its kind in the entire United States. Each young adult with a disability—each "friend"—lives in a suite with three seminary students. There are six suites in the Friendship House building.

The "friends" have the opportunity to live with a great deal of independence and yet have the support of their roommates when necessary. We had been hearing about Friendship House for many months as the development plans were being made and monies being raised to construct the building. Initially, I— notice that it was me!—didn't think Zach was either old enough or ready for this next step, this *really* big step. But God had other plans. As Friendship House was preparing to open, two different people on two distinct occasions broached the subject with me and encouraged us to consider this option for Zach. God was obviously moving, and I needed to set aside my doubts and fears and pursue this potentially life altering opportunity. So I did, and we decided to apply for Zach to live at Friendship House. We talked with Zach about it. He was unsure about the idea but understood that this was the opportunity he'd been preparing for all these years: independence! As a family, we agreed to go through the application process; if accepted, Zach would then be able to choose whether or not he wanted to move there.

We began to complete the application forms, answering lots of questions and gathering information. We were required to find three people who knew Zach well enough to provide a letter of reference addressing his abilities and readiness for independence. We understood the importance of giving an accurate assessment of his capabilities and life experiences.

We talked with Zach through this process, asking continuously for his input. When all the materials for the application packet had been finalized and the letters of reference received, I asked Zach whether he would like to look through the application and read the letters of reference our friends had written. His response: "Sure." He sat down on a barstool at the island in our kitchen and began to read through the letters, one by one, grinning and chuckling, occasionally making comments like "That was nice." It was a delight for me to watch him read, knowing as I did that he was enjoying the stories about himself. He took his time, and when he had finished reading all three letters, he stood up and proclaimed with a smile on his face and enthusiasm in his voice, "I love my life!"

Rick and I were both standing there, and we were amazed at his words, so simple and yet so profound. He has and exercises the ability to see such goodness in his life; he rarely, if ever, dwells on, talks about, or even mentions its sometimes painful and difficult realities. He doesn't feel sorry for himself, doesn't consider himself deprived or express sadness about his "limited" opportunities. I realized that all of these were *our* issues; we were the ones assuming Zach would prefer a different life, the kind of life the world tells us we should all want. These assumptions are irrelevant to Zach, who has an evident zest for exactly the life he has. The world would be a different place if each one of us would carry such a positive attitude about who we are and embrace the life God has give us.

The works of God are truly on display in Zach's life. "This happened so that the work of God might be displayed in his life" (John 9:3). Zach is a young man who is confident in his abilities, contented, and at peace with the man God made him to be. I continue to reflect on and learn much from his exuberance and resilience.

Pause to ponder, praise, and pray

To what degree do the words in Philippians 4:12–13 accurately reflect your daily attitude:

> "I have learned the secret of being content
> in any and every situation . . . .
> I can do all things through him
> who gives me strength"?

Has there been a time when your child's attitude of gratitude has convicted you?

Praise the Lord for blessing "the home of the righteous" (Proverbs 3:33). Then trust Him to do so for your own family home and/or for that of your semi-independent child.

Pray for your child(ren) to grow and develop into all God has created them to be.

> For _____ is God's workmanship,
> created in Christ Jesus to do good works,
> which God prepared in advance for _____ to do.
> (Ephesians 2:10)

CHAPTER 21

I'M
FAMOUS

> *"When people laugh*
> *at Mickey Mouse,*
> *it's because he's so human;*
> *and that's the secret*
> *to his popularity."*

WALT DISNEY

Our time slot for the Friendship House interview finally arrived, and Zach seemed a little anxious about it. Friends at CBI, his education program after high school, wished him well. For "goals" that day at school, Zach worked on interview skills. He was well prepared, and off we went. After we arrived and greeted the selection committee, they began to ask Zach questions. Zach would say that the first question was a "hard" one: "Why do you want to live at Friendship House?" He made it through that one and then was very articulate in answering the other questions and offering information. We stayed quiet. Later in the process the interviewers asked Zach to name a positive quality about himself—something good about Zach. Zach thought about this for only a few quiet moments before responding, "Well, I'm famous!"

"Oh, really!" the committee member responded. "Why?" Zach went on to explain that he had been on TV and on the front page of the newspaper. You know, famous! This was a great answer, and Rick and I couldn't help but chuckle. Zach is overflowing with positive qualities and could have chosen any number of them. Where he came up with "I'm famous!" is anybody's guess, but it was another classic Zach moment—one we'll treasure always.

Approximately two weeks after this interview, Zach received a letter in the mail with the news of his acceptance into Friendship House. We were excited about this unique and wonderful opportunity, yet uncertain about the timing and whether the arrangement was really right for Zach. He was only 21 years old, and we had always assumed he would continue as a young adult to live at home with us. We had even finished a room and bathroom on our lower level so he could have his own space. But now a decision had to be made; we assured Zach that it was his to make and that we would support him either way.

After our initial conversation about his acceptance, Zach didn't bring up the subject at all. Nor did we, knowing that he needed time to process and think. About three weeks later Zach and I were out and about running errands. We ended up at Taco Bell, one of his favorite places to eat. Before we got out of the car Zach voiced a question that had evidently been on his mind: "Mom, if I move into Friendship House, how will I get to Hawkeye football games on Friday nights?" I explained to him that I would drive to Friendship House on Friday afternoons to pick him up and get him to the high school for the game or to catch the team bus for away games. I told him that after each game he could either come back to our home to sleep or we would drive him back to his apartment at Friendship House. That was all Zach needed to hear. His one concern about leaving his home in Hamilton had been resolved. There was no question he knew his priorities.

This step of faith, this release of our son to independent living, turned out to be positive for our budding young man. Zach has grown in his skills of independence far beyond the capabilities we could ever have imagined for him. He manages his own work schedule and his transportation to and from work. He schedules his haircut appointments and walks or rides his bike to the salon. He gets his prescriptions filled at a local pharmacy, pays his rent on time, shops for his own groceries, fixes his meals, and keeps his apartment organized.

This has been a learning opportunity for us too. Rick and I were excited about this seemingly daring experiment, yet we felt uneasy about the many unknowns. We had to release our son to live with complete strangers, young men we'd never even met. As Zach's mom, I was accustomed to helping him keep track of all things; now, in contrast, I was going to be for the most part out of the picture. *What would he eat? Would he be safe walking to where he needed to go? Would anyone notice if he wasn't around or didn't come back when he was supposed to? How would I know whether he made it back to his apartment in the evening? Would he remember to take his medication every day? Get up in time to go to work? Wear clothes that matched and were clean?*

And the list could go on and on. I knew these were, once again, my issues, and that I needed to relinquish Zach and his circumstances completely to God's care. After all, I had been praying all these years for protection, friends, and independence. Now I needed to lay down at God's feet all of my fears. I knew in my heart that, while hard for me, this was best for Zach. I'll admit that I struggled in those early weeks after he moved out. I missed him! But it soon became apparent that Zach was not only managing and surviving at Friendship House; he was thriving.

Four months after Zach had moved into Friendship House, after basketball practice on a snowy, cold Michigan December evening, one of the coaches offered Zach a ride "home." This coach lives in Hamilton, where our home is, and figured he would be kind and offer Zach a ride. During the drive Zach was showing this coach his new iPod touch, but about 10 minutes into the ride Zach looked up and asked, "Where are we going?" The coach responded "to your house in Hamilton." Zach informed him that "home" was his apartment at Friendship House. The coach kindly turned around and drove Zach back to his official—his real—home, his apartment. To be perfectly honest, all of this felt at first a little like a knife in my heart, but deep down I was so thankful our son had moved into this wonderful place that now was truly home.

Pause to ponder, praise, and pray

If you're an empty nester, compare the relinquishment of your special-needs son or daughter to that of any other kids you may have. Do you have a feeling of peace about his/her situation comparable to your assurance that your other child(ren) are safe and well?

If you're still early on in the process, have you been able yet to expend energy thinking about future possibilities?

Praise the Lord for the comfort given by these words of Jesus from Matthew 6:33–34:

> "Seek first his kingdom and his righteousness, and all
> these things will be given to you as well. Therefore do

not worry about tomorrow, for tomorrow will worry
about itself. Each day has enough trouble of its own."

**Pray these verses and trust God for the future of your child(ren),
one day at a time.**

For this reason, since the day we heard about _____,
we have not stopped praying for him/her and asking You,
God, to fill _____ with the knowledge of Your will
through all spiritual wisdom and understanding.
And we pray this in order that _____ may live a life
worthy of You and that he/she may please You
in every way, bearing fruit in every good work
and growing in his/her knowledge of You.
(Colossians 1:9–10)

CHAPTER 22

LIFE
TOGETHER

Co-authored by R. Garret Szantner,
Christopher Billquist, and Kevin R. Slusher

*"God is more interested
in your future
and your relationships
than you are."*

BILLY GRAHAM

L ife in the Friendship House with Zach has been one of the most rewarding experiences of our lives. All of us remember our first time meeting Zach. For Kevin, it was during his undergraduate years at Hope College. Kevin was the student manager for basketball games, and Zach was the manager for the women's basketball team. Garret was first introduced to Zach as he excitedly wrote a message to Garret on Facebook upon learning that they were going to be new roommates. The same goes for Chris. Once you meet Zach, you never forget him—a little shy and quiet, his big smile leaves a lasting impression.

The Friendship House has empowered each of those with special needs who live here to feel real ownership of their respective apartment. This is especially true for Zach. As each of us moved in, Zach was waiting and ready for us. He would clean the apartment in advance for each new occupant and right away begin explaining how life would work for us as residents in the Friendship House. You learned right away that Zach was organized and clean and that we were not to call him by his full name, Zachary Dale—that was for his mother only.

It's hard to articulate what this experience has meant for all of us. Indeed, we are in agreement that our experience at Seminary—training for ministry—would not have been as rewarding as it has been without the intersection of our lives with Zach's. One of his most prominent gifts has been that of joy and laughter. We all have a tendency to take ourselves too seriously; to get caught up in our studies and forget what it is to laugh. Zach has taught us to laugh again; he isn't afraid to laugh at himself or us, and we're all grateful for this gift. In fact, it seems odd to acknowledge how much one benefits from being laughed at. Zach has reminded us what it was like to be as a child, laughing at even the smallest and most overlooked details of life.

The funniest moments of life with Zach come when Zach decides he's had enough of our foolishness. This can take the form of a prank—Zach has been known to freeze our boxers, lock us out of our rooms, or stack the living room furniture in front of your room door at 4 a.m. after all have gone to sleep. We try to fight back but can never out-prank our mischievous friend. On those days when we return from class after a long lecture or receiving a bad grade, when we forget why it is we're truly at seminary or what life is most about—Zach helps us put it all back into focus and live into the wonder of the life God has given each of us.

Another one of the great joys has been Zach's gift of imagination—the key to a life of wonder and joy, as Zach has reminded us. You can have all the knowledge of four years of college poured into your brain, but it's imagination that truly introduces the knowledge to life. Zach has reminded us that when we were children our imaginations knew no bounds. Remember when you would watch a movie as a child and imagine yourself into the story? After it was over you would role-play the movie with your sibling, or simply play all the roles yourself. That's what it's like to live with Zach. Whether he's imagining himself as the King (his hero, Elvis), as Uncle Jesse from the sitcom *Full House*, or when he uses "the force" from Star Wars to open the doors at the grocery store, Zach has taught us once again to dream and imagine, to use our creativity, to fuse knowledge and imagination into a life characterized by serious playfulness.

One of the other important gifts Zach has given to us is that of truth telling. As you grow into an adult, you're often taught to suppress the truth in the name of politeness. Yet as a Christian, you come to realize that true love often requires speaking truth into the lives of others, albeit with gentleness. While Zach may not always share the truth in the gentlest way, he never shies away from letting you know where you stand and what he thinks. This has been refreshing for us. Just as Zach has taught us the humility to laugh at ourselves, so too has he taught us the humility of living in grace and truth with one another (John 1:14, 17).

As we think about all the gifts Zach has brought into our lives, we want to be clear: while we've talked about a return to childlike joy, imagination, and the ability to speak what's on our minds, we're in no way insinuating that Zach is childish. He is most certainly an adult in the full sense of the word—a much healthier adult than most of us are. Zach takes care of himself, holds a job, does his own laundry, cooks, and cleans, and he does this all as the most organized person we've ever met. Once Zach sets a habit or writes something into his schedule, it's immovable. Zach has somehow managed to combine the best of adulthood with the best of a childlike faith, joy, and imagination. Most adults move into adulthood forgetting to bring the best of their childhoods along with them.

We all think one of the most valuable life lessons we've learned with Zach is the reality of brokenness. It's difficult sometimes as Zach may struggle to communicate an idea, as we may struggle from our side to find the right words to communicate something to him, as Zach shares with us his desire to some-day marry and have a family, or as his severe arthritis limits him from putting his electric shaver back together.

Yet there's great beauty in brokenness . . . and it isn't cheap beauty. Zach has helped us to see the brokenness that's part of all our lives—yes, even ours. Zach has taught us that Christ is here in the midst, standing with us in brokenness. As the story of Jesus and Lazarus from the Gospel of John teaches us, Jesus sheds tears as he sees the pain in Mary and Martha after the death of their brother. Our God sheds tears with us, too, in the sight of human brokenness. Yet we know the story doesn't end there and that it won't end here for us in our brokenness. Yet while we're here we're reminded that to be Christian is not to avoid such brokenness; instead, we're led *through* brokenness by our faithful Savior Jesus Christ.

Many people ask us about what life is like with Zach. Often their questions include insinuations about how we're doing some great service or sacrificing so much by living with Zach. These observers remark how wonderful it is of us to teach Zach about life. While we understand these questions and their motivations, the truth is that these assumptions are so inaccurate that they couldn't be further from the truth.

We really can say that we haven't taught Zach a single thing. While we have in some ways sacrificed the freedom of living alone, sacrifice often brings about true joy and true love—greater rewards by far—and living with Zach has done just that. Whether it's the joy Zach brings as we watch him return home from managing the women's basketball team at Hope, riding his bike with the music cranked up and headphones on as he sings at the top of his lungs; the moments of truth when he tells us that "you smell"; those moments when Zach reminds us to use our imaginations as he transforms into the Red Power Ranger; or when we see the deep truth of beauty in all of our broken- ness, life in the Friendship House with Zach has been one of the greatest joys and blessings of our lives.

Of all our experiences of life with Zach, one weekly prac- tice has been the most gratifying. One of the first things you learn about Zach is that he's passionate about cooking. While all of us were lounging in the living room of our apartment dur- ing one of the first weeks of the academic year, Zach eagerly ex- pressed that he not only enjoyed cooking but also had a spe- cialty dish. We enjoyed an excited conversation about Zach's love for cooking and then set aside the ensuing Friday night to indulge in Chef Zach's most exquisite culinary feat—spaghetti and meatballs with meat sauce.

Truth be told, we seminarians had no idea what we were getting ourselves into. Cooking with Zach is a learning experi- ence. Not only does Zach love to cook, but he is so advanced in the culinary arts that he reads aloud the steps of the recipe and directs us both in what to do and how to do it. Zach will occa- sionally step in to show us how something is done, but for the most part he functions as the ever-helpful parental figure guid- ing us kids through the process of "how to cook." On that first Friday night we together refined our skills of boiling water and cooking noodles; making a meat sauce with ground beef, meat- balls, onions, and sauce; and combining these elements into a tasty meal—all under the direction of Chef Zach.

As we sat down to eat we first took the time to give thanks and praise to God for such a good meal placed before us. For this soon-to-be-traditional suppertime ritual, one of us would regu- larly open with prayer and Zach would close. We can't exactly remember what Zach said that evening when he prayed, but we all remember one thing—it was a more profound, theologically based, and faithful prayer than any of us seminarians could have offered. Zach talked to God about what he did during the day, about the good weather and beautiful environment, and about what he planned to do for the rest of the week and a bit into the future; and, of course, he gave thanks for his own cooking abilities.

Together we enjoyed a plentiful dinner—a dinner marked by plenty of good food and great company. No sooner had we put away the dishes than Zach presented us with a question: "So, would you like to do that again sometime?" Thus it began: over the course of the last nine months we made "family dinner" every Friday night at 7 p.m. As we recline in the living room, succumbing to the comatose lethargy that settles over us after eating one of Zach's meals, Zach takes the opportunity of a captive audience to find out exactly what we're going to cook the following Friday. We chuckle and wonder how it is this man can even think about eating at a moment like that. We eventually figure out what it is we'll make, but Zach's habitual question means something more: it provides us with the knowledge that the goodness and joy we shared at the table just moments earlier will soon be ours again.

Zach often says that his time at the Friendship House, managing the Hope College woman's basketball team and working at Culver's, is the living out of his "college years." This is yet another Zach saying that's more profound than what meets the ear. Though we all live together in one apartment, Friday night is the only time each week when all of us come together to share a meal and enjoy together the good food with which God has blessed us. Perhaps the most underrated reason for college being a tough adjustment is that preparing and eating meals becomes utilitarian; the average student sees the mess hall as a place to gain sustenance for daily life. Yet, just maybe, an understanding of the beauty that happens around cooking and sharing a meal is a value that has become lost for more of us than just college students. To prepare and eat food while sharing in the company of others we enjoy is one of the most beautiful parts of life—in our case, something that living with Zach and doing our "family dinner" has forever taught us.

Although many consider Friday nights a time to get out and get involved with some activity after a long week of work and school, there's nothing we would rather do than cook together, share a meal, and learn how to live by living life together. Gathering around the communion table in worship, being met and fed there by Christ in grace, has deepened our sense of what it means for us as roommates to share a weekly meal together. We make time on Friday nights to enjoy the good blessings God continues to pour out upon the world. "Family dinner" is a time to celebrate culinary gifts, the blessing of food, and the joy that comes from the love of a good thing—in this case, the elation of others as a direct result of Zach's passion for cooking.

"Family dinner" has taught us that sharing in the company of others around a meal is not only a gift of grace but also a time of grace in which we learn how to offer prayers that are pleasing to God, to share, and to recognize Jesus Christ dwelling with us in our midst. Because we have dinners every Friday night, we have the ability throughout the week to invite others who don't live with us to come into our apartment and share a meal. Living with Zach is an incredible blessing, one that helps us plumb the depths of life's goodness. We rejoice in our brother Zach, whose love for food and the shared experience of cooking and eating a meal is a gift of grace that embodies the very essence of fellowship in Jesus Christ.

Pause to ponder, praise, and pray

What mealtime traditions for your family benefit all of you far beyond the enjoyment of good food? How did these traditions develop, and what do they mean to you?

Praise God for the reality of Proverbs 15:15: "A cheerful heart has a continual feast."

How true has this been for you and your family? What can you do to ensure that you continue to enjoy this kind of "feasting" together?

Pray for your child(ren)'s relationship with God.

> Merciful Lord, I ask that _____ will love You
> with all his/her heart, with all his/her soul,
> and with all his/her mind.
> (Matthew 22:37)

CHAPTER 23

HOPE COLLEGE
BASKETBALL

*"Don't measure yourself
by what you have accomplished,
but by what you should accomplish
with your ability."*

JOHN WOODEN

Z ach, as I believe I've mentioned (smile!), loves sports, football and basketball in particular. After graduation from high school, he continued on as manager for the Hamilton High School football team. I was taken aback, then, when he announced to me one day, "My dream job is to be the manager for the Hope College football team." Hope is a local Christian college, located about twenty minutes from our home. We didn't pursue this immediately but began to put out "feelers." I talked with people we knew who were involved with Hope, but the door of opportunity just didn't open up for Zach and Hope football.

A year or so later, Zach's Special Olympics basketball team attended a clinic hosted by the Hope College women's basketball team. These young women did drills, shoot around, and then refereed the games for the Special Olympians. They also invited the Special Olympians to attend some of their home games and even provided them with tickets. Zach enjoyed these games, and we went to several that year. Zach had already gotten to know several of these girls through Camp Sunshine. As I sat through these games, I began to feel God nudging me to speak with the Hope women's basketball coach to see whether Zach might be able to help the team even in some small way. With each game I was more and more convicted that I needed to write a letter, and yet I waited. Finally, I knew I just had to do it.

This was a step of obedience for me. I think that, as the parent of a special needs child, I sometimes simply get tired of asking. I'd feel as though there was always something, and often, these being situations in which Zach couldn't completely advocate for himself, I was the one who needed to do the initial asking. When the football idea failed to present itself, I was hesitant to seek and ask yet again. I knew, however, that even if nothing came of the letter, I needed to be obedient and write it. In my letter to the coach I asked simply for an opportunity to meet with him to discuss the possibility of Zach getting involved with the program in even a small way.

The response was immediate and positive. We met a short time later, and Zach was in! Zach himself set up and kept an appointment with the coach. Afterward, he walked out of the field house and exclaimed, "I got the job!" I can't recall when I've seen him more excited about an opportunity. It was at about the same time that Zach moved into his new apartment at Friendship House, so when basketball season began that fall he could walk both to the practices and the games. He immediately felt like a part of the team, and near the end of the season, when the girls won the championship, Zach climbed the ladder to help cut down the net.

Zach wrote the following to one of the seniors on the team after another season had ended:

April 2010

Dear jenny cowen,i will miss you so much jenny cowen you are special to me as a friend and i will always rembber you and you always rembber me too and we always rembber we send time togather and we always rembber that in my whole life and call me sometime once in a while to hangout again real soon if you are not to bus...y. your the best hope college chick your friend Zach Aalderink

Dear Zach Aalderink,

I will miss YOU next year! Thank you for being such a wonderful friend to me, and all of the basketball girls too. I am so happy that I have gotten a chance to get to know you, Zach. One day when you're not working at Culvers and I am done with school, we will have to go for another bike ride . . . sound good? Or we can play some Wii (just NO tennis because you will SMOKE me)! You are an unforgettable friend!

Talk to you soon,
Jenny Cowen

I'm reminded again of how much better God's plans are than what I might have had in mind. It's essential to trust that He knows what's best, both for us and for our children. I may think I do—after all, I am the mom—but ultimately God's way is the best. Take time to get to know God. Spend time with Him. He both knows and will do what's best for our kids, and He won't fail to give you guidance.

My Man Zach and Coach Hayes
By Brian Morehouse,
Hope College Women's Basketball Head Coach

Ever since I met Zach, I've greeted him this way. Not sure why, it's just our thing . . . . But I'm getting ahead of myself.

How did a young man with Down syndrome end up assisting a college women's basketball team? Zach's mother, Linda, contacted me. She explained that she'd heard I had a "heart" for Special Olympians and other young people with physical or mental challenges. Would I be interested in having Zach assist our team? I didn't know how to respond because I'd never met Zach, so I told Linda I'd like to meet him personally and discuss his abilities. As soon as we met, Zach and I connected, and I knew it would work. He was so enthusiastic and professional (even sporting a tie in readiness for his job interview). We discussed his potential role, responsibilities, and guidelines for what would be appropriate in his interaction with our women.

In the beginning we kept it pretty simple. Zach assisted with equipment pick up, filling water bottles, etc. But as we've progressed Zach's role has increased. He's now in charge of the huddle before practice and sending us home after practice. He has also learned to run both the score clock and the shot clock (in fact, he's taught ME how to do this because I'm technology challenged).

Zach has been a great addition to our team. He joined Rich Hayes (we call him Coach Hayes), who has some cognitive development challenges and is fifty-five years old. Together they form the dynamic duo. Rich has been with me for 16 years and really took Zach under his wing. To observe those two laugh, tease, and bicker is a thing to behold! They both have helped assist our team in breaking down the barriers between people with and without special needs. If you asked our players, they would tell you that Zach and Rich are just part of the team. They expect and love their involvement in our practices, so much so that when either is gone, the first question (as it would be with a coach or teammate) is "where's Zach [Rich]?" And you talk about reliable! Both of these guys are at practice 30 minutes or more before we start, pumped up and ready.

Someone asked me last year how it was going with special needs individuals helping out with my program. My response: I can't imagine going to practice without My Man, Zach and Coach Hayes. They make both me and my team better. In no way are they a burden; they're a blessing.

Pause to ponder, praise, and pray

If you've been involved with high school or college sports programs, how would you evaluate the ancillary learning to which you or your kids have been exposed ("life" learning beyond the scope of sports and sportsmanship)? Which emphases would you describe as positive and negative, and why?

Using Romans 11:33–36, praise God for the riches of His wisdom and for His paths that are beyond tracing out. Personalize your praise by applying it in particular to God's dealings with your special child.

Take a quiet break right now and pray for God to equip your child(ren).

> May You, the God of peace, equip _____ with everything
> good for doing Your will, and may You work in _____
> what is pleasing to You, through Jesus Christ, Your Son,
> to whom be glory for ever and ever. Amen.
> (Hebrews 13:21)

CHAPTER 24

RETROSPECT:
THE GOOD
AND THE
NOT SO GOOD

*"When a child is locked in the bathroom
with the water running
and he says he's doing nothing
but the dog is barking, call 911."*

ERMA BOMBECK

Looking back to those earlier years, the beginning of each school year invariably brought new challenges related to adjusting to a new school, teacher, friends, or a different classroom. These factors developed a pattern of misbehavior that I began to see emerge in the fall of each school year. In Zach's younger years the problematic behavior might be as simple as refusing to come in from recess when the bell would ring. One year Zach simply decided that he didn't want to follow the rules, preferring to continue playing on the slide. He figured this was a great opportunity to have the slide all to himself. After a couple of these episodes, the teacher contacted me and asked what she should do. My response: "What would you do with another child with this behavior?" The answer was "pick a brick." The misbehaving child would face the wall near the principal's office and pick a brick to stare at for a predetermined amount of time. "Then have him pick a brick!" I asserted.

The next day at recess Zach again decided that having the slide to himself was a pretty great deal, . . . but this time there were consequences. He picked a brick. And that was the last time he stayed out past the recess bell. He fully understood that he hadn't been following the rules, and he also understood that infractions would lead to consequences. After facing the consequence in this situation, he learned from it.

Isn't learning from their mistakes our hope for all of our children? They all misbehave at one point or another; they need to be taught to follow the rules and be respectful to those with the authority to discipline them. We may feel unsure whether or not they really understand. We may feel that because our particular child has special needs she must be treated "specially" in all circumstances. While I agree with the necessity of taking into consideration a child's cognitive ability and level of understanding, what I have observed the vast majority of time is that Zach did understand and that the consequences for inappropriate behavior were both necessary and beneficial for him. Our gut instinct is to protect—and we must do that—but there's a fine line between protecting and overprotecting, between intervening and enabling.

There were other incidences of misbehavior, especially during Zach's junior high years. Like all boys his age, Zach was growing and changing. He was becoming a young man. And it seemed as though, in conjunction with these changes, he would make a decision at the beginning of each school year to test the limits and see how much he could get away with. As parents we continue to be thankful for teachers, school staff, and friends who spoke truth to him and held him accountable for each incident.

As counterintuitive as this may seem, our children feel secure and loved when reasonable expectations and boundaries are set for them, as opposed to letting them get away with misbehavior; this general parenting principle is especially true with special needs children. We do our children a great disservice by assuming they don't or can't differentiate right from wrong. Life can be challenging enough without adding to it the natural consequences of being disrespectful and disobedient. Kids with Down syndrome do understand and can learn appropriate, rule-abiding behaviors.

It's true, of course, that our kids can be rule followers who mind their own business and still be troubled by negative influences outside our control. This is what I feared most and probably still do. My fervent prayer as Zach entered elementary school was for the other kids to be kind to him. I feared his being teased, ignored, called names, or ostracized during recess activities. I clearly remember an incident when Zach was in early elementary school. One day I observed him walking up our driveway after school. Since I usually walked out to the bus to greet him and say hello to our bus driver, I knew immediately that something was amiss. He exited the bus with the strings of his sweatshirt pulled way to one side. Someone had been pulling on those strings, and it wasn't Zach!

In an attempt to find out what had happened, I asked Zach about his ride home from school. I really didn't get much of an answer, but my mama bear instinct reared up, and I was determined to get to the bottom of this. I knew one of the older girls riding our route, so I called her mom to ask whether she would talk with her daughter. I wanted names! She agreed. What we found out was that there were a few sixth graders on the bus who had been messing with my boy. I followed up with the school principal, who, in turn, did a follow-up with the older boys responsible for the string-pulling incident. Zach was moved to an assigned seat near the front of the bus, and the issue was resolved.

I continue to send up prayers of protection over Zach. This is the only way I know—and I believe the best way—to protect him. As much as we might want to, we can't keep our kids with special needs in a safe bubble in our own home, tucked away from the world. Our kids need every bit as much to experience the world and what it has to offer as do their peers without disabilities, every bit as much opportunity to grow and to be challenged. An overly protective parent can do more harm than good. But we do need to advocate, where appropriate, for our kids.

I learned early on in Zach's educational years to trust my instincts in his regard. There were a few instances when I didn't agree with how a teacher was handling Zach on an academic or behavioral issue. I'll interject here, in retrospect, that these were long and difficult academic years. As I tried to follow my intuition on what was best for Zach, I sometimes clashed with the professionals. I learned through those encounters, gaining confidence as the years went by.

I'm not suggesting or implying that the professionals didn't know what they were talking about. They did. The journey through Zach's formal education was peopled, in my grateful opinion, with some of the best educators on the planet. But placing Zach in a "regular" classroom in a school system with no other kids with Down syndrome was bound to create bumps along the way. Fortunately, none proved insurmountable. They simply required a bit of patience, time, and learning for all concerned. And they required that I, as Zach's parent, learn to advocate effectively for my child—to become confident enough in myself and who I knew Zach to be to appropriately intercede for him.

In addition to the issue of physical protection is the emotional and spiritual protection needed both for our kids and for us as their parents. There's a word still occasionally used—often without forethought or ill intent—that has become offensive to me: it's the "R" word. You know it—retard. Terms change over the years as culture changes, and although we no longer officially use this term to describe our children with cognitive impairments, the word still has currency in society. When you have a cognitively impaired child you come to despise the flippant use of this derogatory term. Even today, 25 years after Zach's entry into this world, it still makes me cringe. The implication and connotation of this descriptor makes is synonymous with "stupid"—and nothing could be further from the truth. Our kids are both bright and smart, and I hope that one day this term will be effectively expunged from use in everyday language.

Curiosity can make us do things we don't intend to do. It's as though we can't help it. I find this when I'm out in the grocery store shopping with Zach. People often stare at him, though I'm not quite sure why. Sometimes it's little kids giving him a second look, but too many other times it's adults. I'd like to ask them about what they're thinking. I usually assume, probably wrongly, that they're looking a bit longer because they're surprised that he's out with me in public. I hope this isn't the case. Or they may be surprised that he's doing his own shopping. Or wondering how he'll handle selections in the store. Are they wondering whether he's really capable to making informed decisions?

I also at times sense a bit of pity toward me, the mom. *"Poor thing, having to shop with her grown son."* Actually, there could be a whole host of reasons for looking askance or surprised. On the flipside of the negative, I myself may be guilty at times. When my husband or I see a child or adult with Down syndrome, we're drawn to them. We love to observe and interact with them. We'd love to sit down and hear their story, knowing we would share much in common.

What I see as a protection in all this is that Zach is almost totally oblivious to the attention. When he's shopping, he's on a mission, and nothing is going to deter him from getting the groceries or other items he needs. He's focused and knows exactly which aisles to shop in to fill his grocery list. It may be indicative of extra sensitivity on my part that I even see the stares. I suppose it's that protective nature God has built into us as parents. I'm thankful Zach isn't bothered by the glances and even the gawks, that he goes about his business just like any other purposeful 25-year-old.

Pause to ponder, praise, and pray

To what extent have experiences of societal/public insensitivity related to your child's disability contributed to the hurt both of your child and of yourself and other family members?

How have you approached the situation, both in terms of your overt reactions/responses and of your own attitude/peace of mind?

Has a stress on forgiveness been important or helpful, both for you and, if applicable to the situation, for your child?

Praise God our protector. Praise Him too for His blessings on those who share in this concern:

> "Blessed are those who have regard for the weak;
> the Lord delivers them in times of trouble.
> The Lord protects and preserves them."
> (Psalm 41:1–2)

Ask God to cover your child(ren) with His protection, today and always.

> Lord, I pray that You'll keep _____ from all harm.
> Watch over his/her life;
> watch over _____'s coming and going
> both now and forevermore.
> (Psalm 121:7–8)

CHAPTER 25

LIVING THE INDEPENDENT LIFE

*"You can change your life
by changing your heart."*

MAX LUCADO

After high school graduation, Zach attended a program in our area—CBI—for teaching life and job skills to young adults with disabilities. He learned a great deal through this practical instruction about how to get around in our downtown, handle public transportation, manage his money, cook, interview, and work at a real job.

Today Zach enjoys his life as much as, and maybe even more than, other young adults his age. In addition to his role as the manager for the Hope women's basketball team, he has a part-time job at a Culver's Restaurant and lives independently at Friendship House. He has come so far from that day in junior high school when he couldn't even pronounce the word "independent," let alone understand what it meant to live it out. Zach has spontaneously expressed to us a few times just how much he enjoys his life. He doesn't get hung up on what he lacks, as we at times tend to do. He looks at life and assesses it from one standard: all that he has. One day a few years ago he expressed to me a wish that he could drive. He had never mentioned this before, nor has he since, but the incident confirmed for me that he is well aware of what others his age are doing and realizes that he can't do it all. Yet he absolutely loves his life and is satisfied with all the opportunities that have come his way.

You may be wondering whether Zach is a rare exception in having so many opportunities and capabilities. I don't believe he is. Many of the young adults I know who have a disability of some sort, including Down syndrome, live full and independent lives. There are numerous fulfilling opportunities today for special needs people, and I believe the possibilities are endless. When Zach was young we didn't see all of this, but as he grew we continued to catch glimpses of what is out there—especially since societal perspectives and expectations have been growing along with our son. We still don't know what the future holds for Zach, but we absolutely know who holds his future. We trust in the One who created Zach—for today and tomorrow and always.

Pause to ponder, praise, and pray

If your special needs child is older, how have expectations, prospects, and societal attitudes changed since he/she was small? If you find yourself in the early stages of the journey, are you surprised and/or pleased by the opportunities available to you as a family? Are you availing yourselves of them?

Praise our gracious God as in 2 Corinthians 12:9–9:

> "But he [Jesus] said to me, 'My grace is sufficient for you, for my power is made perfect in weakness.'"

Pause for a moment to pray this verse for/over your child(ren) . . . and for you.

> May _____ trust in You, Lord, with all his/her heart
> and lean not on his/her own understanding;
> in all _____'s ways may he/she acknowledge You,
> and You will make _____'s path straight.
> (Proverbs 3:5–6)

CONCLUSION

The need for encouragement and hope for families is great. We are living in a time with great pressure on families— their time, their finances, their relationships. Add to this the news that your newborn baby has a disability or the child you are pregnant with has or may have a special need, and the pressure mounts. The long-term prospect of caring for a child with special needs can be daunting. My prayer is that on the pages of this book you have found hope and encouragement that to raise a child with a disability is more than doable; it can actually be filled with abundant blessing, with amazing growth in yourself, with tears of joy and sadness, and with lots of laughs along the way.

What the world sees as disposable, God sees as valuable. He promises a purpose and plan for each of His children, including those—from my experience, especially those—with special needs. How often in the Bible we find that God uses the "least of these" to do His work and show His love. We have experienced this in rearing a child with Down syndrome. My hope and prayer is that you will, too.

The task of caring for all the needs of this child was more than I could face some days in the beginning. It was difficult and overwhelming to look too far down the road. I didn't know what the future would hold, and I wasn't at all sure I would want to know if I could. One day at a time became my philosophy. I knew God would provide mercy new every morning.

I recently learned of a baby with Down syndrome who was adopted by a family nearby. The biological parents were well-educated, Ivy-league people, and when they discovered they were carrying a child with Down syndrome they decided they just couldn't go the distance with him child, so they'd put him up for adoption. This situation is bittersweet for me. That the biological parents gave birth to this child and wanted him well-cared-for is wonderful. I applaud them for the thoughtful decision to give life to this precious child. At the same time, I'm sad for them. They have just given away a wonderful baby who would have blessed them beyond anything they could ever imagine in their wildest dreams! Then, again, I'm excited for the adoptive family, who chose this child and is excited about raising him and the journey it will take them on. I wonder, if the biological parents had heard about or read about a story like Zach's, would it have changed their minds? It might have. It might not have. I would like all parents to be able to make informed decisions, before and after their children are born, to be able to talk to "real" people, people who have "been there, done that." Stereotypes abound about kids with disabilities, and my prayer in writing this book is that we will dispel some of these stereotypes and preconceived notions. Get rid of the myths. All of these children are not alike. They cannot all be clumped into one group of "retarded" or "mentally impaired" or "cognitively impaired." These are simply labels that are given to children to manage them in our educational system. Each child is unique, designed with a purpose and a plan by the Creator. Each one deserves a chance.

We, as parents, all need the opportunity to hear the truth, to be encouraged and given hope for a bright and joy-filled future with our families. My hope is that Zach's story will have touched your heart and given you encouragement and a desire to see each accomplishment of your child and each new day as a precious gift. May you experience immeasurably more joy and hope in this journey than you ever believed possible.

Pause to ponder, praise, and pray

Because of Your great love, O Lord, we are not consumed,
for Your compassions never fail.
They are new every morning;
great is Your faithfulness.
I say to myself, "The Lord is ____'s portion;
therefore he/she will wait for Him."
You, Lord, are good to those whose hope is in You,
to the one who seeks You;
it is good to wait quietly
for Your salvation.
(Lamentations 3:22–26)

Amen! Thank You, Lord!